STOCK CAR TEAM SECRETS

BRUCE MARTIN

MBI Publishing Company

Contents

First published in 1999 by MBI Publishing Company,
729 Prospect Avenue, PO Box 1, Osceola, WI 54020-0001 USA

MBI Publishing Company books are also available at discounts in
bulk quantity for industrial or sales-promotional use. For details
write to Special Sales Manager at Motorbooks International
Wholesalers & Distributors, 729 Prospect Avenue, Osceola, WI
54020-0001 USA.

Library of Congress Cataloging-in-Publication Data

Stock Car Team Secrets: top NASCAR teams reveal keys to
success/Bruce Martin.
    p. cm. —(Motorbooks ColorTech)
    Includes index.
    ISBN 0-7603-0535-8 (pbk.)
    1. Automobiles, Racing—Performance. 2. Automobile driving.
3. Automobile racing. I. Title. II. Series.
TL236.M3517   1999
796.72—dc21   98-46886

On the front cover: A fundamental factor in the formula for
creating a successful racing program is the ability of the crew
chief to motivate his team to function as a cohesive unit. Crew
chief Robin Pemberton motivates his team by being a hands-
on leader. In this shot from the 1998 running of the Brickyard
400, Pemberton rolls the left-front tire from Rusty Wallace's car
out of the way while Billy Wilburn (center) tightens the lug
nuts and jackman Earl Barban waits for the right moment to
drop the jack. *Brickyard 400 © 1998 Indianapolis Motor
Speedway, photo by Jim Haines*

On the frontispiece: Ray Evernham communicating with Jeff
Gordon via the team's two-way radio on race day. Evernham's
main secret to racing success is employing just the right
temperament to get the most of his driver's ability. *Dave
Edelstein, courtesy Indianapolis Motor Speedway*

On the title page: One of the biggest advantages a crew chief
can have is possessing a sense of when to take a gamble. This
is one gamble, however, that failed. Dale Jarrett's crew pushes
the Quality Care Ford Taurus back to its pit area after it ran
out of fuel while leading at the midway point of the 1998
Brickyard 400. Jarrett had dominated the race up to that point
and the mistake may have cost him over $1 million. *Photo by
Jim Haines, courtesy of Indianapolis Motor Speedway*

On the back cover: What secrets could these two top
NASCAR Winston Cup crew chiefs—Hendrick Motorsport's
Ray Evernham (right) and Roush's Jimmy Fennig (left)—be
sharing, or are they just reliving old contests in this candid pit
view? *Photo by the author*

Edited by John Adams-Graf

Designed by Pat Linder

Printed in Hong Kong

Dedication

This book is dedicated, in part, to the mechanics of NASCAR Winston Cup racing who work long, hard hours to fulfill their dream of working in the sport they love. Also, I would like to dedicate this book to my family and friends for their support in this project and in my career.

Acknowledgments

Just as a NASCAR Winston Cup driver cannot get into victory lane without the help of his team of mechanics, an author cannot write a book alone. This book could not have been produced without the help of crew chiefs Ray Evernham of Hendrick Motorsports, Robin Pemberton of Penske Racing South, and Buddy Parrott, general manager of Roush Racing. These three men were generous with their time, and they allowed open access to the race shops where the cars are prepared for Jeff Gordon, Rusty Wallace, Jeff Burton, and Mark Martin. Special thanks also goes to crew chiefs Todd Parrott of Robert Yates Racing and Jimmy Fennig of Roush Racing (who call the shots for drivers Dale Jarrett and Mark Martin) for allowing the author an inside look at prerace preparations.

Team owners also played a role in the production of this book. They include Richard Childress, team owner for drivers Dale Earnhardt and Mike Skinner; Michael Kranefuss, team owner for Jeremy Mayfield; Don Miller, one of the co-team owners for Wallace; and Jack Roush, who owns the cars driven by Martin, Jeff Burton, Chad Little, Johnny Benson, and Kevin Lepage.

Thanks to Jay Signore and his staff at the International Race of Champions (IROC), who provided time and assistance for the chapter devoted to IROC. And thank you to the many drivers who took time to be interviewed for this project.

A special thanks has to go to Kevin Davey, licensing director of the Indianapolis Motor Speedway, and Ron McQueeney and his fine photo staff at the Indianapolis Motor Speedway, for providing images that appear throughout this book.

Those pictures not shot by McQueeney's staff were shot by the author, which presented a special challenge to someone who makes his living with a tape recorder, laptop computer, and an inquisitive attitude, rather than behind the lens of a camera.

Thanks also to Steve Zepezauer, editor of *Circle Track Magazine* in Los Angeles, for his advice. Also, thanks to Michele Spagnola of Kodak Premium Processing in Fairlawn, New Jersey, and the staff at Lakeside 1-Hour Photo in Cornelius, North Carolina.

Photo editing and advice were given by Kurt Hunt of Indianapolis, Indiana; Peter Wozniak of Milwaukee, Wisconsin; and Ron LeMasters, editor of *National Speed Sport News* in Harrisburg, North Carolina. The final photo editing was done by the author, who owes thanks to Corinne Economaki and the staff at *National Speed Sport News* for use of the publication's photo department.

Special thanks to Bob Zeller (Zippy), formerly the auto racing writer for Landmark Newspapers and the author of books on Mark Martin and Jeff Gordon, for his advice and countless hours on the telephone with the author.

And thanks to Jim Morganthaler, the executive editor at ESPN SportsTicker, for his patience and understanding while I was attempting to complete this book and manage my "day job" at the same time.

Hopefully, the readers of this book will gain insight into the role of a crew chief or top mechanic on a NASCAR Winston Cup team and be entertained at the same time.

Bruce Martin

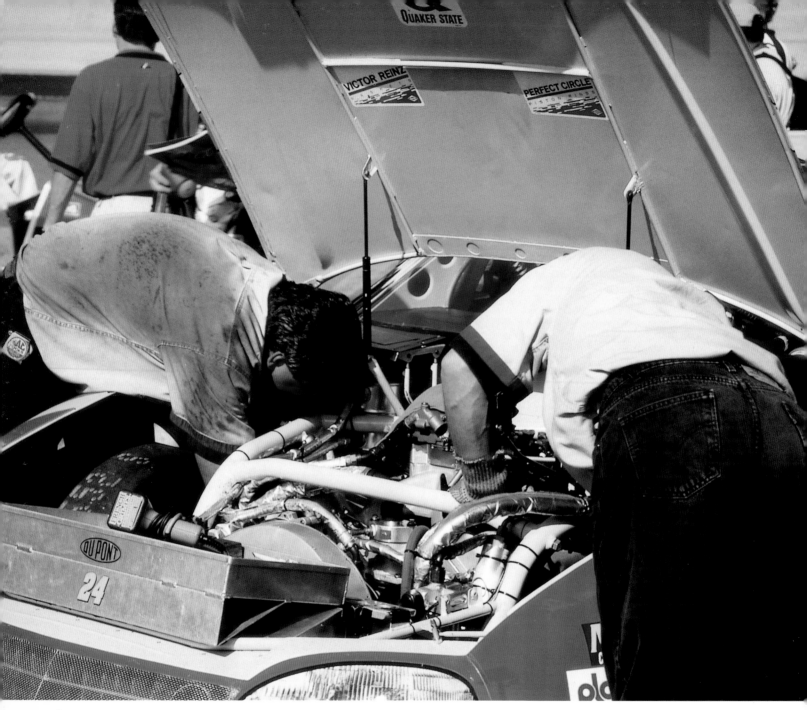

Before a car competes in a race, there is plenty of hard work involved. Two of Jeff Gordon's crewmen prepare the DuPont Chevrolet Monte Carlo before a practice session at Bristol Motor Speedway.

The life and reputation of a race car driver are on the line in every race, even though he is driving a machine that was meticulously prepared at the race shop. After a race, the driver's job is over—he is either celebrating a win in victory lane with his crew or leaving the track to recover for the next race the following weekend.

For every racer who has driven into victory lane, there is a crew of mechanics who helped him get there. And while the driver gets the glory, the crew members are the ones who toil the long, hard hours to prepare a car capable of victory.

Some race car mechanics go on to reach the highest rung of the stock car racing ladder—working for a NASCAR Winston Cup team. These top mechanics enjoy fame similar to that of winning drivers. But for most, being a Winston Cup mechanic means long hours worked in anonymity.

The very best mechanics go on to become crew chiefs, forging a special relationship between the crew and the driver. A crew chief has to be an expert mechanic, chassis specialist, engine builder, and race strategist. He also has to possess the unique quality of being a psychologist. He must motivate and lead. Not only does he decide which car to take to the race track, he also has to manage personnel, schedule test dates, and deal with sick days, workmen's compensation, and vacation time. The crew chief rarely gets a day off. He sacrifices his personal life and family to fulfill his dream of working for a race team. It's often a 13-hour-day, 7-day-a-week job filled with the pressures and demands of building a race car that satisfies the driver as well as the team owner and the sponsors.

"I wouldn't want to swap jobs with the crew chief," said Ernie Irvan, driver of the Skittles Pontiac. "Obviously, the driver has a tough job. But the crew chief has a tough job, too. His neck is on the line. The driver has danger, but the crew chief has a different kind of danger." Crew chiefs are a special breed. The long hours don't bother them because they are doing what they like to do best.

Ray Evernham, crew chief for three-time NASCAR Winston Cup champion Jeff Gordon at

This is what it's all about: Hendrick Motorsport's crew chief Ray Evernham celebrates the team's second Brickyard 400 victory in five years with driver Jeff Gordon in victory lane at the Indianapolis Motor Speedway in 1998. *Photo by Leigh Spargur, courtesy of Indianapolis Motor Speedway*

Hendrick Motorsports, said: "It's a mechanical guy's world. Since the Wright brothers built the first plane, somebody has been looking to make it better. It's our challenge. There will always be developments; there will always be somebody trying to invent a better wheel. That mechanical ability and a guy who is willing to work—that is great, because no matter what they do or how many rules they come out with, there is always something you can work on. You can massage the car; there are a lot of areas out there that people are still going to be able to work in. What is neat about racing is

that you can't teach yourself to be a better driver than Jeff Gordon, but you can certainly teach yourself to be a better crew chief than Ray Evernham."

Top drivers in NASCAR Winston Cup racing realize that despite all their talent, they are only as good as the cars they drive. "When you are running good and in contention for the championships, it seems like you are always getting along good with your crew chief," Jeff Gordon remarked. "All of a sudden, when you aren't running good, it seems like the guys aren't getting along with their crew chiefs." This crew chief-driver relationship is essential to Gordon's winning formula. "I love the relationship Ray and I have," Gordon said. "It's funny because if it wasn't for racing, I'm not sure if we would actually get along real well because we are kind of opposite. What racing does is bring us together. He pushed me in the direction I need to be pushed in and I push him in the direction he needs. Sometimes he is too intense and sometimes I'm not intense enough. We really make a great team when it comes to that."

For each winning team, the formula of the success is complicated, and often hangs on one key element. Gordon summarized the essential element of his special driver-crew chief relationship: "Respect is the biggest thing I see. We all have a lot of respect for our crew chiefs and that also comes back to the crew chiefs having a lot of respect for their drivers. You don't see us bad-mouthing them or telling them what to do, but you do see us working real hard and trying to make things work. No matter what the situation, no matter if you are the slowest car on the track or the fastest car on the track, you are always trying to get better and better. The only way that is going to happen is to work well with that crew chief. Every year, it gets more competitive. More teams get better, drivers start to come in to their own and start jelling with their crew chiefs and teams."

Mark Martin has been at Roush Racing for more than a decade. He understands just how important the crew chief is, especially in a series where the race cars are so equal. "I think everyone in racing knows how much of a team effort it takes," Martin said. "You have to have that bond with your crew chief to get the results you want. Everybody has the same stuff. My car (a Ford Taurus) is just like Dale Jarrett's. We have access to the same stuff—the same shocks, the same chassis, the same body. The rules are so tight. We can't build one better than theirs, and they can't build one better than ours. So then, it all comes down to the people—what they do with the material they have. I've got a great relationship with Jimmy Fennig and I have also had the luxury of a tremendous relationship for 10 years with Steve Hmiel. All of us are pulling as hard as we can to make this thing work and put that car out front every week."

Martin points out that the fundamental factor in success is the ability of his team to function as a single, cohesive unit. "If we are on our own, we are only as good as ourselves. Each one of us relies, more than I can tell you, on our crew chiefs . . . If we were standing out there by ourselves, we would be in trouble. That's why I rely on Jimmy, Jack Roush, and all our guys. Each guy on the team is an expert in some area of the field. Each one of these guys happens to be smarter than me in his particular piece of it. Whatever it is that he does, he does it better and knows more about it than I do. We all know that. You are always going to have that [in a good team] and hopefully those guys respect their driver and think, 'He's the man.' The driver is going to have the same feelings for his team if he is getting the job done."

Dale Jarrett drives for one of the most innovative and motivated team owners in the sport—Robert Yates. Jarrett has also developed a strong relationship with his crew chief, Todd Parrott. The drivers go out of their way to commend the men who build them a race car capable of winning.

"It's all about people," Jarrett said. "It doesn't matter what business it is, our business or the business you are in or anything else, it's about surrounding yourself with the right people. I think Ray Evernham, Jimmy Fennig,

or Todd Parrott, there are a couple things you find in all of them. One, we all have a respect for each other. We all show that respect and we all have confidence in each other. That is key in this sport—to have confidence in the guys you work with.

"The other thing is, 95 percent of the time, you see the top crew chiefs talking to their crew people and to the drivers, where others are watching another race or getting out of here early. These guys are still around, working. It's not just because of the championship. This started a long time ago. A lot of people work extremely hard in this, but the dedication and desire it takes to be at the top of this sport is not something everybody has. They take the knowledge they have and they put it to good use every single week."

Jarrett does not limit the credit, however, solely to crew chiefs. "The other thing they do is they surround themselves with good people. That has been the key in our organization. Todd got the people he wanted, who could do the best job working with him and around him, working with me. That has made everything click. You see that in the other top teams, also; they have people they can work with and work around and get the most out of. That is a big key along with the determination and desire they have." This sense of overall team commitment transcends the season: "Each race is a championship and this is made up of 33 weeks of championship races. You do the same thing every week. We are all racers and our teams are racers and we are going to come here and win the race, regardless of the situation."

The insights that the crew chiefs, mechanics, and drivers share in this book reveal the heart and soul of NASCAR Winston Cup racing. As Evernham said, "It is a mechanical guy's world." By taking a behind-the-scenes look at the mechanics and crew chiefs in NASCAR Winston Cup racing, fans and Saturday night racers alike will learn many of the best-kept secrets of this extremely popular form of American motor racing.

Communication is one of the most valuable tools of any successful race team. Bobby Labonte discusses the car with his crew chief, Jimmy Makar, following a Winston Cup practice session.

Chapter One

The Key to Winning: Communication

Just as communication is one of the most important aspects of any sport or business, it is the key to successful racing. A good level of communication between a driver and his mechanics can be the difference between winning or losing, whether in NASCAR Winston Cup racing or at the local short track.

The first step to achieving this winning level of interaction is to ensure that the crew chief and mechanics are properly communicating and understanding the driver. A crew that works together and is totally committed will be far more successful than one in which crewmen have independent ideas and work with separate aims and goals. The driver also has to have total trust in his crew chief and mechanics because the decisions made in the pits can greatly enhance or ultimately hinder a driver's ability to win a race. "The crew chief and the driver have to speak the same language," said Ernie Irvan, driver of the Skittles Pontiac. "We all speak English, but everybody speaks a different type of English. The driver and the crew chief have to relate in understanding the feel in a car. If a driver says it is loose, that doesn't mean to tighten it up 100 percent; sometimes it may mean only tightening it up 10 percent. Those are things you have to get out of the driver—what he really wants. When it all comes together, and a team goes on a winning streak, it's almost as if the team is in 'the zone.'"

NASCAR star Jeff Gordon agrees: "I definitely think you can get into a zone," Gordon said. "I feel like I'm driving better than I ever have before with more confidence than I ever have before. It is important for me not to let that confidence grow into overconfidence, because when you get overconfident, it will bite you. And you start to lose respect for the speed and the car and the track you are at. The whole team is in a zone right now. It seems like if I make a mistake on the race track, losing a couple of positions, or Ray and I can't get the car just right, the pit crew makes up for that lost time. If the pit crew makes a mistake or has a problem in the pits, it seems like Ray and I are able to make up that time on the race track. That whole team chemistry is what is

Jimmy Spencer discusses race setups with two of his crewmen in the garage following practice. Spencer has earned the nickname "Mr. Excitement" because of his personality and aggressive driving style.
Photo courtesy of Indianapolis Motor Speedway

building for us right now. That is what is in the zone right now. I don't feel like I could be in the zone by myself. I have to have something to drive, something to pull into the pits and have a good pit stop, for me to be in the zone."

Throughout any race, Gordon will communicate information back to his crew chief, Ray Evernham, in the pits via two-way radio. Evernham uses that information to determine if he needs to make any chassis adjustments during pit stops. If Gordon complains the car is loose, Evernham may elect to make a chassis adjustment by adding more or less weight to one or more of the four springs. A crew member will use a socket wrench to adjust the springs on the front and rear of the race car. Similar adjustments are made with tires by increasing or decreasing air pressure.

"He doesn't really talk to me much on green-flag laps, especially if I'm in a battle with someone else," Gordon said of Evernham. "He talks to me more under caution. If it gets exciting and he hears it in my voice, then he will talk to me. I have to be focused on this race car and communicating with Ray. That is what makes us such a great combination. For a lot of guys out there, it is hard to find that type of relationship and confidence that goes back and forth."

Gordon and Evernham are often able to anticipate what the other wants because of the level of communication they have forged through years of working together. They have been together since Gordon's debut in 1992 in NASCAR Winston Cup racing. They teamed up when Gordon began in the NASCAR Busch Series. If a driver switches teams, the driver and crew have to start all over to learn each other's traits and idiosyncrasies. Sometimes it can take nearly a full season before a driver and crew reach the same level of understanding.

Ernie Irvan can vouch for the time it takes to bond with new crews. After driving for Robert Yates Racing for almost five years, Irvan joined the Skittles Pontiac team for the 1998 NASCAR Winston Cup season. At Yates,

Irvan had worked with crew chiefs Larry McReynolds and Marc Reno. Now, his crew chief is Ryan Pemberton, younger brother of Robin Pemberton, the crew chief for Rusty Wallace at Penske Racing South.

Although Ryan was just starting his second season as a Winston Cup crew chief, the combination was fair at the beginning of the 1998 season. But the two really began to click in August, when Irvan won the pole for the Brickyard 400 at the Indianapolis Motor Speedway and, two weeks later, for the Pepsi 400 at Michigan Speedway. "It's real hard to say everybody is going to be the same when you switch teams," Irvan said. "When I started driving the 28 car for Robert Yates, it seemed like me and Larry McReynolds hit it off right off the bat. That doesn't mean that Larry was a better crew chief than Ryan Pemberton. What that means is at that time, their stuff was really good. Obviously, I knew how to drive and when you put that relationship together, you can go fast. I think we keep working on the Skittles Pontiac all the time, and we keep getting it better."

Upon further reflection, Irvan added, "I think we were clicking right from the very start, but we weren't performing like we would like. When you start running good is when people think you are starting to click, but I thought we clicked right off."

As one of the newer crew chiefs in NASCAR Winston Cup racing, the 29-year-old Pemberton brings a fresh approach to the race team. The 1997 season was Pemberton's first as a Winston Cup crew chief, working for driver Derrike Cope, who was replaced at the end of that season by Irvan.

Irvan explained some of the differences of starting with a fresh crew chief: "Ryan hasn't really 'Been there, done that.' There are new ideas we will try with different things. I'm real bad to want to try something off the wall and he keeps me in line. He has to make sure it is good for the whole day instead of just part of the time. Sometimes, a driver/team relationship can stagnate and that is what happened with me at Robert Yates. If you are there

Team owner and crew chief Andy Petree stands on top of the team transporter and uses his stopwatch to time the laps of his driver, Ken Schrader, during a practice session.

Using the information he has gained from the stopwatch, Petree leans into the window of Schrader's Skoal Bandit Chevrolet Monte Carlo to discuss the way the car is performing. *Photo by Steve Ellis, courtesy of Indianapolis Motor Speedway*

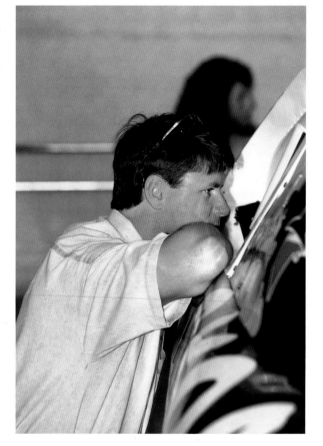

for a certain amount of time, each person has to be open-minded. Just because we did it this way last year doesn't mean we have to do it this way this year. You have to be able to advance with the times. That is what we are doing with this team, advancing with the times."

When Irvan drove for Robert Yates, he was living in Mooresville, North Carolina, and the team was based 40 minutes away in Charlotte. Now, Irvan is driving for a team that is located in Mooresville, 5 minutes from his house, which makes for a quick trip from home to the shop and improved communications throughout the week. "I come in once a week and go over what we need to do for the next race and look back at what we did the previous week," Irvan said. As he spoke, he reflected momentarily on the many facets of Pemberton's job and said, "I really respect the job the crew chief has to perform." He elaborated, "Each crew chief only has 24 hours in a day, and each guy treats the amount of time he has to spend on every piece of the race car differently. Ryan stays focused on his job. That is something that will pay off at the end."

Irvan's former teammate, Dale Jarrett, works with crew chief Todd Parrott at Robert Yates Racing. Jarrett and Parrott are both second-generation racers. Jarrett's father, Ned, won NASCAR championships as a driver in 1961 and 1965. Parrott's father, Buddy, has been the crew chief for some of the top drivers in NASCAR history and is currently the general manager at Roush Racing. Jarrett and Parrott begin talking about a race well in advance of when the team departs for the race track. "We'll talk Monday or Tuesday or sometime the weekend prior to the race," Parrott explained. "We'll sit down and get one race ironed out, then talk about what we want to do next week. That way, we'll go into work on Monday and I'll have an idea and understanding of what we are looking for the following week for the setup.

"My goal and the way I look at things are a lot different than other crew chiefs or other people. Some of them will look at four or five races down the road, which we prepare for. But mentally, in my head, I try to take it one race at a time because I think you can get your mind so scattered, you can't concentrate on what you want to do." Parrott has determined his own winning formula, "I'm not sure how my dad does it, but I try to take it one race at a time, one week at a time, because it is a long, busy schedule with a lot of travel. I have family at home and I like to spend time with them. If you get too much on your mind, you can't think about the important things in life."

Mark Martin's crew prepares the Valvoline Ford Taurus prior to a race. Every nut and bolt is tightened, and the crew gives the car a thorough inspection before it goes through NASCAR technical inspection.

Crew chiefs Jimmy Fennig and Ray Evernham share a laugh during
one of the many long days at the race track.

The night before, or the morning of, the race, Parrott will go to his office in the back of the team's transporter, where he can be alone with his thoughts and plot the strategy for the race. "I guess I'm different, I kind of wing it," Parrott said. "There are certain places we do have strategies, fuel mileage races and things like that. A place like Bristol, 500 laps, anything can happen on any given lap. You just race the race. We know how far you can go on tires on fuel mileage. If the caution comes out, you know you want four tires. But if you haven't run very long, you may stay out because track position is very important. There are so many different ways to approach your race car, you have to give it what the driver is asking for, the feel he is looking for. I think the biggest thing, more than anything, is the driver feel. Some drivers like the race car to be a little free, a little loose; some don't like it to be free."

The crew chief of any top-level race team approaches his job the same way as the head coach of a football team. He spends many hours preparing for the next event, and then it's a matter of reacting to how that event plays out. "You are organizing and directing all these guys while trying to end up in the same place," Parrott said. "It's fun. It's a challenge."

Mark Martin first worked with Jimmy Fennig when Martin was driving in the American Speed Association (ASA) in the mid-1980s after his first effort in the Winston Cup Series, in 1983, failed. Martin returned to Winston Cup as a driver in 1988 and was reunited with Fennig when Jimmy was hired as his crew chief in 1997 at Roush Racing. In two years, the pair formed one of the best driver/crew chief combinations in NASCAR. "Mark and I work out OK," Fennig admitted in his characteristically understated fashion. "We both talk about things and changes we want to make. He'll think of something, I'll think of something, we'll talk it over, and we'll do it. We worked together for two years in ASA. Bobby Allison drove for us back then and Rusty Wallace used to drive for us."

Fennig spends much of his time, however, communicating with the crew rather than with the driver. "If you treat people like you would want to be treated, you will get more out of them," Fennig said. "You don't need to work the hell out of them. If they are working on that car pretty good and they get the stuff done, they need to be rewarded, too. That keeps morale up and keeps everybody pumped up."

Before a race, a crew chief will work with the crew on the setup of the race car—perhaps the most important session for the mechanics of the entire weekend. Any mistake will show up quickly once the race starts. "You go over every nut and bolt, every nook and cranny," explained Robin Pemberton, Wallace's crew chief. "You take some of the running gear out and look at it. Everything that moves on the car gets a wrench laid to it or an eye on it. You always need more time than what they give you, and you use everything they give you. It's a three-hour process, getting ready."

Pemberton believes he has an advantage because his driver, Rusty Wallace, has a tremendous understanding of every aspect of the car's chassis and is able to communicate that back to him. Behind the wheel, Wallace is meticulous and calculating. "That is what makes him a good race car driver," Pemberton said. "When you are in the race car and trying to do all your things, you know the good and the bad that can come out of any event. Everybody is coming with a common goal, which is to win the race. We have had bad stops, good stops, and trouble with the car, but there have only been a couple of times that he has been upset with the race car. He gets focused, and he knows what is going on."

An age-old question in auto racing is "Which is more important, the driver or the car?" If a team hopes to win, the answer is that they are equally important. But it is an equation that is always in flux. "It changes from track to track," Evernham said. "I tell people that every week. At Daytona and Talladega, the car is a bigger part of it than the driver. At Watkins Glen, Martinsville,

Two of Sterling Marlin's crew members at Sabco Racing in discussion during the 1998 Brickyard 400. *Photo by John Schmidt, courtesy of Indianapolis Motor Speedway*

Darlington, places like that—the driver is a bigger part of that than the car. At Indianapolis, there you have to have a 50-50 combination. The car is a big part because of the horsepower and aerodynamics, but the driver has to be pretty smart there, too. Again, there are certain places where you don't have to have a spectacular chassis setup, you just have to have a car that works. At Watkins Glen, give them good brakes, give them a good transmission, and get out of the way. There, it is a lot of driver."

A driver's background can have a big influence on how quickly he learns to read and feel and communicate that to the crew chief. Jeff Gordon came from open-wheel racing in the United States Auto Club (USAC) midget, sprint, and Silver Crown series. He adapted to stock car racing very quickly. "I don't know if Jeff's open-wheel experience helped him understand the car, but a race car is a race car and tires are tires and a guy who has a good feel for car control is going to have that," Evernham said. "Car control—that is something all these kids doing go-karts and quarter-midgets and little minisprint things are learning. They are learning how to race. Whether they are going to drive or not, who knows, but they are going to be good crew chiefs and mechanics because they are learning how to race. All the 90 races or whatever Jeff did in sprint cars and midgets didn't do anything but teach him car control. He knows, 'OK, I can't do that or I'm going to spin out,' or 'I can do that without spinning out.'"

Currently, no pair in the Winston Cup Series is communicating better than Gordon and Evernham. Their record is proof of that. "There is no argument with the combined ability of Jeff Gordon and Ray Evernham. For the time and the place, they are the perfect combination," Irvan said. "There is no way you can argue that. Right now, they are doing everything right."

But communication is only one of many elements that make up a winning race team. In this increasingly technical sport, a team must have the right tools to put itself in a position to win . . .

A member of Mark Martin's crew at Roush Racing gets instructions through his headset during a race. *Photo by Dave Edelstein, courtesy of Indianapolis Motor Speedway*

Crew chief Jimmy Fennig looks into the video monitor to watch the race on television. The pits offer one of the worst views at the race track, so team members install television sets with their toolboxes in the pit area. *Photo by Tim Holle, courtesy of Indianapolis Motor Speedway*

Robin Pemberton, Rusty Wallace's crew chief, in a conversation with David Smith, a crew member for driver Mike Skinner at Richard Childress Racing.

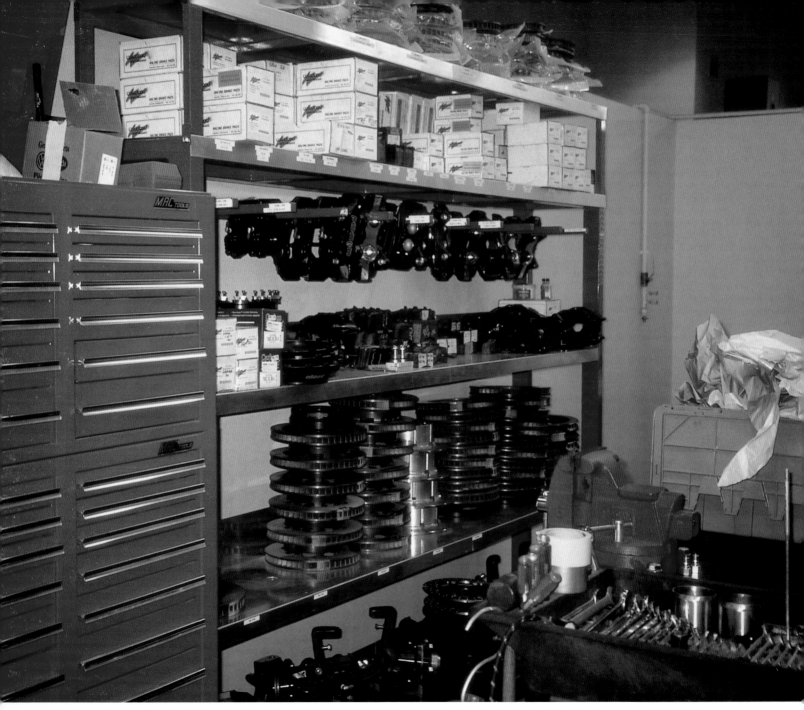

Here is an expensive collection of brake rotors and brake pads at the DuPont Racing Shop at Hendrick Motorsports. Jeff Gordon depends on these brakes to help keep him out of trouble.

Chapter Two

The Tools of the Trade

A visit to any NASCAR Winston Cup or Busch Series race shop reveals tools of all varieties—tools that are essential to a NASCAR Winston Cup team. If a race driver is only as good as his race car, then the race car is only as good as the mechanics. And no mechanic is able to do his job without the proper tools. Nick Ollila, engineer for Penske/Kranefuss Racing, which owns the cars of Ford driver Jeremy Mayfield, remembers the days when tape measures accurate to a sixteenth of an inch were the epitome of accuracy in stock car racing. "And it's not like I'm that old either!" said Ollila, a 44-year-old native of Detroit, Michigan, who has been on national championship teams in NASCAR and Indy car racing.

Today, crew members use tools such as the Computer Numerical Control (CNC) machinery. This device, which is constantly being refined by Hardinge, the manufacturer, has made machining parts for NASCAR cars as accurate as a surgeon's laser. "With CNC, we can take a part we need, draw it up on a computer, feed it into a machine on a disk, and it converts it to machine code," said Ollila. "The machine can then select the tools it needs, the cutting speeds which will work the absolute best, and determine the path the cutting tool will take. It's amazing. Once the part is drawn up, virtually all you have to do is feed the machine the materials and it does the rest."

Like many Winston Cup teams, Penske/Kranefuss uses the CNC with a three-access lathe with live tooling and a vertical-machining center. These two machines, coupled with Hardinge's CNC, enable the team to build virtually identical chassis parts, one after another. "You build your own chassis so you can control the material, the quality of the construction, and the geometry," Ollila said. "It makes an incredible difference for a race team, which we've seen this year. CNC enhances all three of those areas. You can set the brackets, pedals, suspension points, spacers, and everything else on the chassis, and every one is exactly the same. How much of a difference does that make? You start stacking up all

The race day toolbox for driver Rusty Wallace and the Penske
Racing South crew. Tools and parts are here for virtually every
conceivable thing that might need replacement during a race.

These are tools a team hopes it never has to use. A variety of hammers and saws are in the toolbox at all times to pound out damage that might occur in a race.

the tolerances while building a car without CNC on a car over 200 inches long, and every car is going to be radically different. You'll have one car 198 inches long and another 200 inches long. Two inches is a tremendous difference on a race car. Before CNC, a really good machinist—and I mean a really *good* one—could, on a good day, come to within a couple thousandths of an inch on a part. Hardinge's CNC increases that tenfold, at least."

The CNC provides two essential elements—precise accuracy and speed. "Take an upper control arm plate, for example," Ollila said. "A man on a hand machine could make 50 of them in four or five days, and every one of them would be just a little bit different. With this CNC, you can make 50 of them in half a day and they are exactly identical."

Perhaps the newest tool that has had the biggest impact on racing is the shock dyno. The latest, cutting-edge area that race teams work on is the technology of shock absorbers, because they greatly affect the performance of the race car. "There was a car owner I worked for about 15 years ago, Bob Rahilly," recalled Robin Pemberton. "He and I laugh about it today. We were trying to really get onto the shock deal, and he told me once, 'You could take every shock that everybody owns, put them all in a big pile and go there and pick four shocks out, and it would be no different than what you tried.' That was when we were starting to really learn Bilstein shocks and Delco shocks. Penske shocks weren't around yet. We look back at that and laugh at how far the shock program has come. Everybody gets to buy the same pieces. The difference is in the people bolting

Back at the race shop, plenty of tools and toolboxes are used to build a top-level Winston Cup race car.

Springs and shock absorbers are important items that help control the handling characteristics of the race car.

them together. For four years now, we have had Tom Hoke as our shock guy. He was with Bilstein for many years. Even though we have a sister company in Penske shocks, we don't have any more technological advantage or ability to know any more about it than anybody else."

Ray Evernham is largely responsible for developing shock absorber technology in Winston Cup and showing how important it is to a winning race car setup. "When we first came into this sport, I think we had an advantage because not a lot of people were into shocks," Evernham recalled. "They would bolt them on, but because of my involvement with Penske and knowing and understanding the Penske shocks, we got on top of it pretty good. Now, everybody has a shock guy. Shock technology is going to explode. When I first started doing it four or five years ago, everybody thought it was pretty tricky. Some of the stuff these new guys are doing really blows me away, and it's just growing and growing. It was an area that was pretty easy to get an advantage in, but now it is not because everybody has

Legendary driver and now full-time team owner Richard Petty sits atop the toolbox and uses a stopwatch to time his driver, John Andretti, during a practice session at the Indianapolis Motor Speedway. *Photo by Leigh Spargur, courtesy of Indianapolis Motor Speedway*

jumped on it, and some pretty smart people are involved in it."

Someone not in the sport may ask "What makes the shock absorber so important?" Evernham is quick to point out, "The shock controls the car by controlling how fast the wheel moves. What you are trying to do is change that control by changing the shims in the shock. You can add and subtract little metal washers that add or reduce the amount of force it takes to push that shock. A shock controls time. Your spring controls the weight, but your shock controls time. You are not only trying to control how much grip that wheel has, you are trying to control how fast everything moves. You are trying to control time with that shock."

Dale Jarrett and his team at Robert Yates Racing also place major emphasis on shock technology. "We work awful hard on the chassis and on the shocks that we run," Jarrett said. "We have a really good guy in Chris Hill, who works our shocks." Jarrett has realized that the interplay of shocks with the chassis is a major key to winning. "Whoever can conserve their tires the best will be good in the race. More times than not, you will have long, extended green-flag racing. That is what we work and plan for. That is the way we approach every race. Some guys in Happy Hour (the final Winston Cup practice) throw on new sets of tires and run and use up two or three sets. We run the same set of tires all afternoon. We will start on a new set, and run 70 laps or so. That is how we find out if the setup is good enough for the long, extended runs."

The radial tires on a race car become a tool themselves, as crew members make air pressure adjustments to improve the car's performance. "It's a tool, there is no doubt," said Evernham. "I don't know if it is the ultimate tool. Certain guys have certain tools, but it applies more to the situation you have. You can't say air pressure is the best tool every Sunday because it is not. At Michigan in August 1998 (where Gordon won), air pressure didn't mean anything because we were up and down

Seventy-five rear-end gears, at $2,000 each, line the walls of the
rear-end department at Hendrick Motorsports. These rear ends are
used in Jeff Gordon's Chevrolet Monte Carlo.

Air guns, impact wrenches, and power sanders are all valuable tools
for any race mechanic.

Race-ready shock absorbers line this bin in a race team transporter. Shocks are extremely valuable for setting up a competitive car, and their numbers are among the most guarded secrets of a race team.

and all over with it. It happened to be a spring rubber that was the key at Michigan. To me, the most important tool setting up the car on Sunday is information. Everybody has a different philosophy based on it." The information is useless, though, without Evernham's most crucial element. Surprisingly, he does not hesitate to share his secret weapon. "I can show you my most important tools: My team—my guys—are the key to winning. The rest of the stuff, everybody can get. I can get a stopwatch just like Jimmy Fennig, but why did he beat my butt so bad on Saturday night? It wasn't

the stopwatch. We carry the same tools as everybody else. We use a lot of paperwork and we use a lot of organization, but to me, my tools are the people. I guarantee you, if you look at the top 10 in points, the cars are almost identical—the springs, the shocks, the whole deal."

Evernham and other crew chiefs pick the best cars for each particular track through testing or by studying their records on how a certain car performed in previous races at that track. Sometimes, a team will build a brand-new car and hope for the best.

Ernie Irvan's crew chief, Ryan Pemberton, sits atop the toolbox while one of his crewmen uses a pair of binoculars to get a better view at the Indianapolis Motor Speedway. *Photo by Mag Binkley, courtesy of Indianapolis Motor Speedway*

Everything that goes to the track is loaded onto the team transporter, which is essentially a traveling race shop. "We will take both cars, the primary and the backup, three engines, and enough parts on the truck to build another car if you had to," Evernham said. "We have support carts, toolbox with the tools, scales, cool-down units to help get the car qualified. Gears, transmissions, springs and shocks because we have so many different combinations that we could go to. The track could change—it might be tight then loose. Tracks like Darlington and Rockingham are always way different in the fall than they are in the spring, so we have to carry tons of gear ratios, transmissions, springs, and shocks, besides the mechanical parts. Our crash cart is pretty complete, too. We have not run into a situation where we didn't have the part we have needed."

Obviously, the best tool for any race team is the driver. The driver provides some of the most valuable input from behind the wheel. "The driver, in my opinion, is more than just a driver," said Jeff Burton, one of the five drivers at Roush Racing. "Because of the way Winston Cup racing is, the driver is the brain of the race car. Only the driver can relate to the team what is going on in the car on the race track. Nothing else can do that. If you have an education in racing, and you put in time and you understand race cars, you can provide information to the team about how to make the car better. That is what I try to do. I try to help build better bodies, help with the springs and shocks, and build better chassis. I'm lucky enough to have a team that lets me do that. Some teams don't let their drivers get involved in it, but my team wants me involved. Mark Martin's involvement really helps us. We are two drivers who like to know what is going on and like to have input in it."

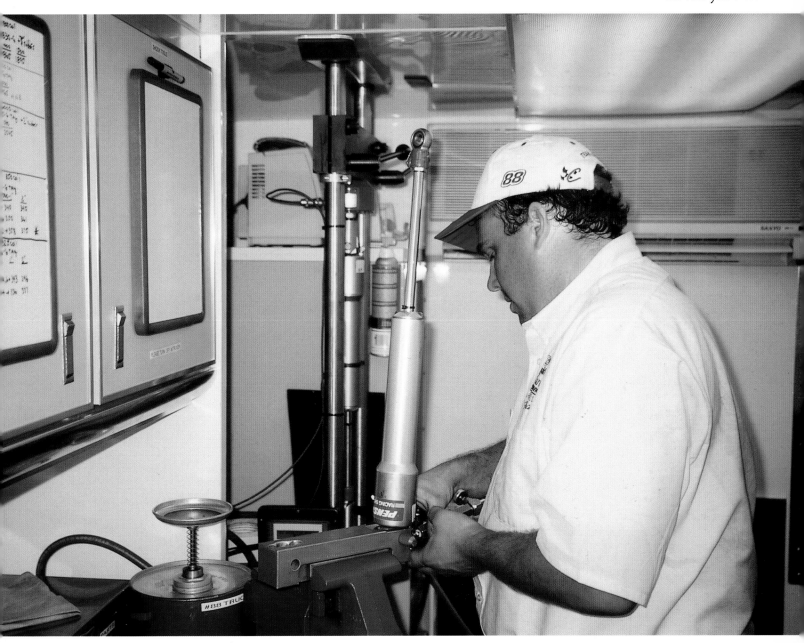

Shock specialist Chris Hill works on the shock dyno in the team transporter for Dale Jarrett's Quality Care Ford Thunderbird at Robert Yates Racing. *Photo by Mag Binkley, courtesy of Indianapolis Motor Speedway*

Power steering pumps line the shelves in another part of the massive Hendrick Motorsports complex.

The parts room at Hendrick Motorsports. The value of the parts in this room is extraordinary, but all the parts are here for a championship-caliber Winston Cup team.

Brake calipers at Hendrick Motorsports. The calipers are high tech, in order to slow a 3,500-pound Winston Cup stock car at race speeds.

In the shock room at Hendrick Motorsports, more shock technology is put to use to help give Gordon a winning setup.

Ray Evernham in the transmission room at Hendrick Motorsports, looking over another valuable collection of transmissions for his race cars.

40   Brooke Gordon, Jeff Gordon, and Ray Evernham celebrate in victory lane at the Indianapolis Motor Speedway in 1998, after Gordon became the first two-time winner of the Brickyard 400. *Photo by Jim Haines, courtesy of Indianapolis Motor Speedway*

Chapter Three

Ray Evernham: The Psychologist

Of all the crew chiefs in NASCAR Winston Cup racing, perhaps the brightest is Ray Evernham of Hendrick Motorsports. Even if Evernham isn't the brightest, he is certainly the most successful—he has built a NASCAR Winston Cup dynasty with driver Jeff Gordon. Evernham's success is twofold: In addition to possessing a tremendous understanding of interaction of the chassis, the engine, and the shock absorbers, he is "The Psychologist" of Winston Cup racing. Those who listen to the team's radio during a race will attest that Evernham is a master at coaching his driver.

"I always rely on Ray for a lot of things," Gordon said. "I think he can see when I'm really battling hard out there. There are times when he knows he needs to just not say anything and there are times when he sees or hears me get excited and he knows he has to calm me down. It's no different than if something happens on the track or in the pits, and I can hear him get excited. I can calm him down. What makes

the team so great is we rely on each other in the best of times and in the worst of times. Right now, I feel we are communicating better than we ever have. That chemistry is really stronger than it has ever been. He keeps me focused when I get off track, and I keep him focused when he gets off track." Evernham provides Gordon with the confidence he needs to be the best driver in NASCAR Winston Cup racing today. "If there is going to be a cross word said between us, on the radio in the middle of the race is not the time for it," Evernham said. "My job during the race is to help him get in the right frame of mind to get the job done. Screaming at him because I think he did something wrong or him screaming and at me would be counterproductive. It's not what we are there for."

Besides calming his driver, Evernham must keep him focused as well. "My job isn't just being a crew chief, calling the shots and determining when we are going to pit, but also to be a calming force for him and to give him the information he needs to focus on getting the job done. Sometimes things create

On race day, Ray Evernham communicates with Gordon on the team's two-way radio. Evernham is a master at handling his driver with just the right temperament to get the most from his ability. *Photo by Dave Edelstein, courtesy of Indianapolis Motor Speedway*

distractions for the driver. Whether it is the car not handling right, somebody doing something to him on the track, or he gets hot or gets carbon monoxide, I have to take those distractions away and let him know I have the problems handled." Evernham is quick to add, "Even if I don't, I have to tell him, 'It's not a problem. Don't worry about it, I've got it handled.'"

One of the reasons Evernham has the ability to handle a driver is that he used to be one himself. Evernham was known as "Hollywood" when he was a NASCAR-modified driver from New Jersey. After that, he went to work for Jay Signore at the International Race of Champions (IROC) as a mechanic and crew chief. The popularity of NASCAR lured Evernham and his family to the Southeast, where he has become one of the great mechanics in recent NASCAR Winston Cup history. This early experience has been the foundation for making him as famous for his ability to motivate as he is for his chassis setups. "I started to study a lot of coaches," Evernham explained. "Before I decided to come to Winston Cup, I wanted to analyze what it would take to do it better than everybody else. I asked myself, 'What would the keys be to get an advantage if you didn't have a lot of experience?' I approached this the same way a professional sports franchise would be put together. I wondered, 'If a person was going to start a football team, what would he or she do?' I started to study some of the good coaches. Vince Lombardi, also a New Jersey native and buried just around the corner from where my wife's dad is buried, was a natural starting point for me.

"One thing led to another," Evernham recalled. "I was always interested in the business side of things, so I have tried to come up with a combination that would cross business and racing. The biggest key to all of that was understanding that it is all in the people."

Evernham studied and studied and studied, not just racing, but other aspects of life. "I study a lot of the people who have been successful. I try to pick up different things from different people. I've read a lot of business books like those written by Ken Blanchard and even Bill Parcells. Additionally, I remain involved with New Jersey Nets Coach John Calipari—he actually owns the rights to the term 'refuse to lose.'"

Evernham's path to NASCAR Winston Cup racing actually began with the late Alan Kulwicki, the 1992 NASCAR Winston Cup champion who was killed in an

Ray Evernham, in his office at Hendrick Motorsports, discusses race car preparation during one of his many 13-hour days at the shop.

airplane crash the year after he won the championship. Kulwicki, who had a degree in mechanical engineering from the University of Wisconsin-Milwaukee, understood virtually every aspect of the race car. But Kulwicki's brilliance often led to clashes with his crew members. "Two people convinced me I needed to move down here: Alan Kulwicki and Norman Negre," Evernham recalled. "I went to work for Alan, but Alan's personality and mine did not hit it off. Alan was absolutely, positively, without question the smartest person I ever

met in my whole life. But I could not get along with him, nor could he get along with me. We split up."

Following that, Evernham found a new place to continue his career. "Many think I was the crew chief on the Baby Ruth Busch Grand National team for Jeff Gordon at Bill Davis Racing in 1992, but that is not true. I was just one of the guys who worked on the car. Bill Davis and I set the cars up for Jeff Gordon and the Baby Ruth team for 11 or 12 races. Dennis Adcox and I did most of the work on the cars. We won some races

Evernham, sitting atop the toolbox at the Indianapolis Motor Speedway last year, oversees all aspects of the pit crew and conducts race-day strategy for Gordon. *Photo by Tim Holle, courtesy of Indianapolis Motor Speedway*

This loyalty enables Evernham and Gordon to maintain the communication that is essential for a winning team. "He approaches every single race with the same intensity he showed in the Coca-Cola 600 in 1994," Evernham said, reflecting on Gordon's attitude. "Even though he shows up on Friday wanting to win a race, I have never seen him not really be upset if he didn't win. After a poor finish, he can say, 'Gee, we got a good finish. We finished fifth and that was good.' He will go to his trailer to kick and scream. He does not like to lose, but I don't worry about him losing intensity as long as there are other mountains to climb and if he keeps showing up at the race track like that."

Despite the strong connection between Gordon and Evernham on the track, Evernham is quick to admit they have little in common other than racing. "To me, that's enough," he said. "We are complete opposites except for racing. Maybe that is the best thing. He fills all the needs I've always had in my racing career, and I feel like I fill all the needs he has in his racing career. That should be enough."

Evernham is driven, often possessed, when it comes to his race car. But he has been so good at delegating additional responsibilities to members of his crew that he often finds himself thinking he needs to do more. "One of the keys that I've discovered is that I've been very good at being able to delegate authority. Some days, I almost feel lazy," Evernham said. "I try hard to keep my mind clear to constantly improve the team and the car. When I delegate, it gives my team members a chance to be part of what is going on, plus it gives me more time to concentrate on trying to make the team better. I don't spend all my time concentrating on making the car better. I'm also thinking, 'How can I help this guy learn? How can I make the travel better? How can we do things differently?' Nowadays, I spend most of my time trying to improve on what we already have. There are 35 people on the team, including my part-timers and my road crew. The shop is 15,000 square feet with 19 people here every day, not including my secretary and me."

Evernham has plenty of advice for aspiring Saturday night racers. He used to be one himself. "The first thing to remember is never let anybody tell you that you can't do something," Evernham said. "If I had listened to all the people who told me somebody from New Jersey was not going to make it down here, I would still be in New Jersey."

To Evernham, success is more than nuts and bolts. It is intelligence. "Everybody is always looking for a spring or a shock or another trick. If you do want to improve your Saturday night program, you have to realize that it is none of those things. It is organized information. You have to build an information base to make the right decisions. If you have an organized note-keeping process, you are going to be better than everybody else, because you are going to have more information. That may mean investing in a computer." Evernham, however, is quick to admit, "I'm not really computer literate. I have three engineers on this team who are really highly involved in computers. In my era, it was a notebook. The important thing is that you just have to keep track of everything. You have to know every change you made every week and what it did, what it didn't do, all the mistakes you made so you don't make them again. You have to just keep building that information base and keep trying new things just to see what they will do."

Although Evernham has an enormous budget to work with at Hendrick Motorsports, he acknowledges that Saturday night racers have to do the most with the least. "I think most Saturday night racers have a cost limit," Evernham said. "The key to that, though, is for the promoters and people who organize the races to take out the money factor if they really want to have good races. The biggest things a Saturday night racer is going to spend money on are engines and tires, because everything else, a normal mechanical guy can make. If you can weld and fabricate, you can build, repair, or fix just

about anything else. Engines and tires are the high costs in racing for every one."

Evernham advises the Saturday night racer to be judicious with what budget he does have. "Everybody has a budget and that is it. Sometimes, fixing an old part will pay off more than buying a new one," Evernham said. "The Saturday night racer has to set priorities of what is important and make everything else work. Without question, he has to have the right things for safety so he doesn't tear the car up or hurt himself. If he has a bent header, he can fix it himself and save the money. A new right rear tire will let him go faster than how much a bent header is going to slow him down. He has to be able to put those things in priority and put the dollars in the right places."

The struggles of the Saturday night racer to make ends meet is a bit different than Evernham's duties at Hendrick Motorsports, especially when it comes to money. "We have airplane travel, per diem, extra crew members, and rental cars," Evernham said. "The cost of racing is high. You cannot race a Winston Cup event for less than $100,000 a race. That is not including all of the buildings and daily operation expenses. You spend $100,000 a weekend." Nevertheless, Evernham is quick to point out that on any level of professional racing, a smart businessman can make money. "I don't think there is any single secret to this," Evernham notes. "The biggest money in this sport is made in merchandising, not racing the car."

The next career step for Evernham may be team ownership, in which he would be in total control of his racing operation. "There are lots of different reasons why people own cars," Evernham said. "To me, if I wanted to own a team, it would be so I could be in control. The money doesn't interest me. If I wasn't losing money and I could make a decent living, I'd be happy.

Evernham uses his race-day notes and a lap speed chart to monitor performance of Gordon's DuPont Chevrolet during a race. *Photo by Dave Edelstein, courtesy of Indianapolis Motor Speedway*

One of Jeff Gordon's Chevrolet Monte Carlos being prepared in the race shop.

I want to win races. There are some people in this business who don't care about winning races, they care about making money. Again, different reasons for owning race cars motivate people, but in this business, to make big money, you have to win. If all you are worried about is winning, you are going to make money. But if you start in this business and all you want to do is make money, you aren't going to win, which means, in the long run, you aren't going to make money."

Evernham's pay could be described as comfortable; as a Winston Cup crew chief, he earns a six-figure salary. Nevertheless, it's not the money that motivates him. "I'm going to tell you—God strike me dead as I sit here—I never started in this business to make money," Evernham said. "Since the first time I ever worked on a race car or came to Winston Cup, it has never been for the money. I've made a lot of money. I bet I'm as well paid as any other crew chief in the business. But if you

Evernham is big on motivation, as the words on the wall will attest. The Indian he is posing next to is part of the team's nickname, "The Rainbow Warriors."

CHECKLIST

☑ From Nobody To Upstart

☑ From Upstart To Contender

☑ From Contender To Winner

☑ From Winner To Champion

☐ From Champion To Dynasty

Warriors never quit. They know that they haven't failed until they quit.

Warriors are positive – not negative. They think about how they will make it work versus why it won't work.

Warriors hate to lose! They know that friendly, honest competition is fun and profitable.

Warriors say what they WILL DO. Then they do what they said they would do – no fear, no failure, no excuses.

Warriors are happiest and most productive when surrounded by a productive, positive environment. They know that they own creating that environment.

said to me, 'You can make 10 times more money than you are making now, but you are never going to win again,' I'd tell you to stick it. When I moved down here, I lived in a one-room apartment in Concord, North Carolina, where the bed folded out of the wall, at $350 a month. You can't do this for money. If you do, then shame on you!"

Evernham clarified his position this way: "What I thrive on is the competition. I want to prove that I can do it better than anyone else. That is what it's about to me. I want to build a car that is going to beat every other car. When I leave on Sunday and my car has beat 42 other cars, more often than not, people are saying, 'Man, those guys are good.' Look at the money people have spent trying to accomplish that. You can't buy those results with money. Love us or hate us, that is something you can't put a price on."

Evernham is thankful for what he has attained in racing, despite the time away from home and the pressures of battling for a Winston Cup title. He is able to deal with his fame in a humble manner, "I thank God for it every day," Evernham said. "It's something you always hoped could happen to you. I sign autographs with a smile and appreciate it. To me, it's an honor to be in this position. I know there are a lot of people who really don't care for Ray Evernham. But, there are also a lot of people who respect what I am doing and send the team cards and letters and come to visit us. My notoriety certainly is not at the Jeff Gordon level. But then, Jeff is certainly not at the level that Elvis Presley achieved. The bottom line is that we do have some people who think enough of us that they want to take our picture and ask for an autograph. I'm honored by that."

This checklist inspires Evernham's crew at Hendrick Motorsports.

Rusty Wallace's crew chief, Robin Pemberton, at 42, is already a 20-year veteran mechanic in NASCAR Winston Cup racing.

Chapter Four

Robin Pemberton:
Be in the Right Place at the Right Time

Robin Pemberton's career in NASCAR Winston Cup racing began because he was in the right place at the right time. As a teenager growing up in the upstate New York town of Malta, he met one of the true legends of NASCAR racing. It was a meeting that would change his life. "Our family had a restaurant in upstate New York in Saratoga County," recalled the 42-year-old crew chief, who has worked with Rusty Wallace at Penske Racing South since 1995. "Richard Petty stayed across the street from the restaurant and a friendship developed. This was in 1969, when NASCAR was running in Malta at the Albany/Saratoga Speedway. We used to attend races all the time."

The friendship grew and Pemberton's family kept in touch with Petty through the years. When Petty's son, Kyle, began his racing career in 1979, Pemberton learned of a crew opening from his boyhood friend, Steve Hmiel. Hmiel had left upstate New York earlier to join Petty's team as a mechanic.

"I was 23 in 1979, when I moved to North Carolina," Pemberton said. "There happened to be an opening for somebody to do nothing in particular—possibly be involved in doing some work on the cars. It was a big gamble for them to allow me to go to work there, and it was a big gamble for me to pick up and move. It was really exciting. I didn't worry about the money or anything else. I did it for the experience of doing it. That is where the sport was then."

Pemberton did any and all jobs at Petty Enterprises. He began to play one role after another until he was finally a co-crew chief with Larry Pollard. "It was by sheer luck—it wasn't by determination," Pemberton remembered. "I was fortunate through the misfortunes of others. I started working in the fabrication shop. I was always able to move into new positions when somebody else quit and left a spot open, sometimes temporary and sometimes full time. Someone would say, 'We don't have a guy to fill this in. Get Robin to do it until we find a guy.' I got good experience at a good place. It was probably the best teaching place in all of racing history at that time.

Now, that place would probably be Hendrick Motorsports. I was fortunate that they were patient."

Because he worked at Petty Enterprises when Richard Petty was still at the peak of a driving career in which he won 200 races, Pemberton is a bridge that connects the sport's historic past to its explosive future. "The sport has made an incredible change during the last 20 years," Pemberton said. "For example, we never thought about flying to races back then. I don't think I started to fly anywhere until the late 1980s. We drove to the few West Coast races. One time, Kyle Petty, my younger brother, Randy, and I wanted to run Riverside, California. Richard said, 'You can run Riverside, but I'm not paying for any tickets. If you want to go, you have to drive.' So we piled in the van and drove."

It wasn't just the travel arrangements that were different back then, either. The way a team allocated equipment has changed quite a bit, as well. "The maximum number of cars we had for the whole year was three," Pemberton said. "You would run the same car, 8 to 10 weeks in a row. A team didn't build a special car for Martinsville, Sears Point, Riverside, or anywhere. Back then, in 1981, we barely had the resources to build a special car for Daytona. We had a bunch of drivers who ran limited schedules with 16-race deals. Today, we have to run every race."

The size of the fleet of cars was not the only area to expand. "Engine programs cost more now than the entire racing program used to cost, by a long shot. Back then at Petty Enterprises, there were 18 people for two complete race teams. In 1983, I shared crew chief roles at Petty's team with Larry Pollard. We were the two mechanics and we assembled the car. When we went on the road, it was Larry, Richard, a truck driver, and I. The pit crew would be guys who volunteered to come in for the weekend. Now, one complete race team has 55 people."

After several seasons on Petty's team, Pemberton found himself on a trail that carried him to a variety of teams. "I went to Butch Mock's for a year. This was when they didn't have a sponsor and Dave Marcis drove. Butch was the crew chief and I was the second guy. After that, I was at DiGard with Bobby Allison. It wasn't long, though, until I left there and went back to work with Butch Mock and Neil Bonnett for 1 1/2 years. In 1987, the Roush program began. I started there in August of that year and remained until 1991, when I went to Sabco."

Entering the 1998 season, Pemberton had prepared 16 cars that went to victory lane. His best season to date was two years prior, in 1996, when Rusty Wallace won five times. "It was pretty exciting," Pemberton remembered. "At the time, Rusty was winning a lot of races. Me being competitive, I was interested in how a person wins that many races. I wanted to know what makes a team go like that."

Pemberton said now that the sport he entered in the late 1970s has exploded into a major industry, it is tough to keep up with its pace. "If anybody is honest with you, they will tell you that 10 years ago, it used to be a lot more fun than it is now," he said. "And 20 years ago, it was four times the fun. But we weren't as responsible then as we are now. Dale Inman and Bud Moore have to be more responsible now than they were then, and the same thing for the rest of us. You are responsible because of the larger sponsors and the high television viewership. It's real important because of the image we project. With that comes a certain amount of stress about what people think you are and not embarrassing your sponsor. The fact is, it's a lot harder racing now than it used to be. If a person knew then what they know now, 10 years ago they would be winning 20 out of 30. A 15th-place car in the points right now is a far better car than the championship cars of 15 years ago. We keep raising our own stakes. If one team puts engineers on, then everybody has to have engineers. Then you have to have the best engineers. The drivers are the most important element, though. You really have to try to keep the drivers happy. They make or break you."

A Penske South crew member performs race-day preparation on Rusty Wallace's Miller Genuine Draft Ford Taurus. The crew member checks off items on the preparation checklist taped to the rear quarter panel of Wallace's car.

As the crew chief, Pemberton has to be present every single day, whether it is at the race track, at another speedway for a test session, or in the race shop where he works long, hard hours with the crew. "That's hard," Pemberton said. "There is not really an opportunity to get away from it at all. You never get a chance to break it up and do something else. If I was going to give any advice to a mechanic who wanted to get involved in this business, I would say, 'Be ready to work long and hard hours. Get with a team that races for a living. That way, everything you do is race-oriented.' The other bit of advice that I would give is, 'You have to start from the bottom up. There is no job too small when you start out at the bottom.'"

55

Earl Barban reaches for a tool as he stands inside the wheel well of
Rusty Wallace's Ford Thunderbird. Barban and other team members
are performing final preparations on Wallace's car before the 1998
Goody's Headache Powders 500 at Bristol Motor Speedway.

In addition to being a mechanic, Pemberton has to deal with the team's personnel details. "That's all the time," Pemberton said. "And I have to always remember that these aren't 9-to-5, 5-day-a-week guys. I have to be flexible. These guys are giving more to the company time-wise, so if they need time off or a day off to do nothing and they think they need it, then they have to have it. The worst thing you can do is get 100 percent of the work out of the people in the first eight months of the year, leaving nothing for them to grab during the last four months of the year. Being very flexible is important. You don't want people to be irritated at work. They need to know that if their kids are sick or if they have something to do that requires them to cut out a couple hours early, they can do it. I figure they have worked more than a couple hours late in the past so it is no big deal. That is how I try to work with my people."

Managing many personalities has its challenges. "It's a concern to some that crew guys may be disloyal. My philosophy is, 'You have to take your personal differences out of it if you are going to be a team.' A football team is 45 players. Those guys don't like everybody, but when the whistle blows, everybody is pulling in the same direction. That is the way it has to be here. With 55 people, you aren't going to find that many people who like each other all the time. But when you get to a race track, they are all pulling in the same direction. That is the competitive nature of people."

Although he has been a crew chief for much of his career, Pemberton has also performed every element of a pit stop at one time or another. "I've done everything," Pemberton said. "The thing I enjoyed the most was changing tires. The hardest part for me was jacking the car. If you are the tire changer, you have to hit five nuts off, five nuts on, four times on a stop. That is pretty physically demanding." Another position on the team that required Pemberton's physical strength was gas man. "Twenty-two gallons of gas is about 78 pounds per can. You have to have a guy with real good upper-body strength who is agile and can run with that can three or four feet one way or the other when the car stops. It is no picnic when you go across the wall."

By ascending through the ranks himself, Pemberton has developed empathy for each of his team members. He clearly understands the dangers. Although he still looks young at 42, Pemberton has plenty of battle scars from his days in the pits. "You get burned all the time," Pemberton said. "I have scars from brake rotors up my arms throughout the season. You just get burned. There were times you used to burn your hands changing tires. You would be done with a tire change and you would have blisters up and down your hands. Being burned is just a part of being at the race track. You physically sacrifice. You will be an old man and you will have all these scars going up and down on the insides of your arms. Hopefully, one day, they will eventually go away. But you aren't worried about that. It's the end result that you are worried about and whatever it takes to get there."

As further example of this sacrifice, "My knees are shot," Pemberton said. "I've been scheduled for knee surgery for two years now, and I keep putting it off. There is no time. I'll be laid up for four to six weeks after I get it done. The guys who won't wear their knees out are the guys who are a little bit shorter and a little stockier. My legs are long and have a lot of stress turning on them. Besides banging your knees on the ground, there is a lot of stress. In the old days, the guys didn't wear kneepads, and the pit stops were 24 seconds long. The impact wrenches are the same as they were 20 years ago, but the stops went from 24 seconds long down to 15 1/2 seconds today. That is a big decrease in time and that is because of the athleticism of the pit crew members. It's like being a wide receiver or a defensive end. You are constantly running hard around the car, turning and twisting."

Being in charge of one of the best-funded, highest-profile teams in the sport at Penske Racing South makes Pemberton's job a little more enjoyable. "I believe this is

One of Robin
Pemberton's crew
members adjusts a
digital satellite dish
atop the team's race-
day toolbox. The dish
picks up the television
feed of the race so
team members can
keep track of areas
of the track they
cannot see.

a good company," Pemberton said. "This company does better by people than a lot of other companies. We fly better when we can. We stay in nice hotels. The travel aspect makes it less painful. And when you have a driver who can win races, that keeps people happy. Some people still just want to win races. I might be able to go to another team and make a little bit more money, but I wouldn't want to be fixing a wreck every Monday. It's nice to know you can go to victory lane any week, and that is important to people."

Two Penske South crew members work on the shock dyno inside the team's transporter. Wallace and his crew are leading innovators in shock technology.

The chassis of Rusty Wallace's car, minus the engine, is worked on at the race shop in the Lakeside Business Park in Mooresville, North Carolina.

The bare chassis of a NASCAR Winston Cup race car before it is
turned into a racing machine at the Penske Racing South shop.

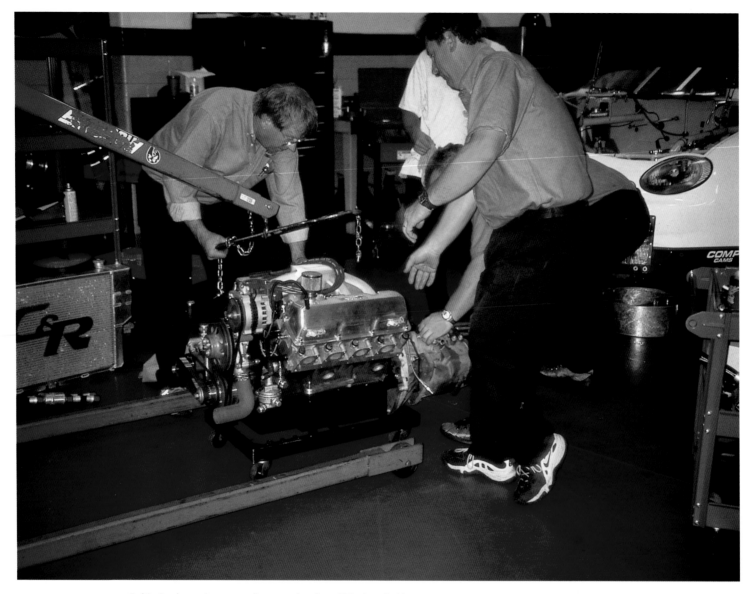

Robin Pemberton's crew readies an engine that will be installed in
Rusty Wallace's Miller Lite Ford Taurus at the race shop.

Joe Lewis, the truck driver for Penske Racing South, puts parts inside the team's test transporter. The team owns two transporters—one that goes with the race team to the races and another that goes to race tests.

Pit crew members in action at the Indianapolis Motor Speedway. Note the body damage on Geoff Bodine's Ford Taurus.
Photo by Dave Edelstein, courtesy of Indianapolis Motor Speedway

Chapter Five

Secrets of Balancing Handling and Horsepower

The speed of a race car is not always entirely determined by the amount of horsepower produced by the engine. To go as fast as possible, a car has to remain balanced through the corners and stick to the track. "If your car isn't handling right, it won't do you any good," said Jimmy Fennig, crew chief for Mark Martin. "You have to have everything these days, because the competition is so close. You have to have horsepower and you have to have handling."

During the course of any NASCAR Winston Cup race weekend, the terms "tight" and "loose" are commonly used by crew chiefs and drivers as each team tries to adapt the chassis to fit its driver's particular racing style. But what exactly do these terms mean? Why do some drivers prefer a loose setup while others strive to be tight?

A tight race car does not want to turn in the corners. The front end moves toward the outside wall. This is also known as "push." By contrast, a loose race car turns easily, but the rear end tends to slide toward the wall in the corners. Ideally, most drivers prefer a neutral setup, one in which the car is neither tight nor loose. However, throughout the course of a race, the driver may want the car to be tighter or looser, depending on the track conditions.

In general terms, looser is faster. This is why certain drivers prefer to have their car on the ragged edge of loose. Mark Martin likes his car set up to go fast. "I like mine loose because I can give it gas when I want it and I can point it where I want it," he said. "I don't have to wait, and that is good—I'm not much of a waiter! Some of these other guys are a little more patient and will take a different approach and still manage to get the job done."

Martin believes he has to scare himself to have an outstanding qualifying lap. He has to take the car to the edge, to the brink of being out of control. The ability to control the car at that level of performance is the difference between a winning driver and one who hits the wall. "If you are loose, then you either wreck or scare yourself," Martin said. "If I get my car loose enough, I scare myself on a regular basis."

Tires are one of the most important tools when it comes to the
handling characteristics of a Winston Cup race car.

Richard Childress, who owns the race cars driven by Dale Earnhardt and Mike Skinner, thinks a neutral setup is best. "Drivers just don't like a pushing race car," Childress said. "They would rather have a car that is neutral or free. Nobody can go real fast with a real loose race car. You just burn the right rear tire off of it, and you don't go anywhere. However, some drivers, Dale Earnhardt among them, can drive a loose race car and get more out of it than the average driver," says Childress. "If a driver has a loose race car, he gets more out of it by staying on top of the steering wheel and sawing the hell out of it. Dale will stay on top of the wheel until we get it in there and get it fixed."

Childress and his crew chiefs, Kevin Hamlin and Larry McReynolds, are responsible for setting up the cars for their respective drivers, Earnhardt and Skinner. "They are real similar in the way they drive, but the problem is Mike doesn't have the experience Dale does, so he tries to set his car according to how he likes the feel at these new tracks," Childress said. "In general, both of them can drive a pretty loose race car."

Buddy Parrott, general manager at Roush Racing, who oversees the teams for Martin and Jeff Burton, has worked with some of the greatest drivers in NASCAR history. "You have a lot of drivers like Darrell Waltrip, who could take a car a little tight with a little push in it and do a lot of business," Parrott recalled. "Dale Earnhardt, on the other hand, would take a car that was loose because of his dirt track experience, with the tail hanging out a little bit, and Earnhardt could get it done."

Jeff Burton prefers a tight car to a loose setup, Parrott said. "Jeff is a guy who loves the car neutral, and sometimes we can't get that," Parrott said. "Jeff can take a car that is a little tight and do more business with it than he can if it is loose. What we do now is try to get the cars at an optimum setup, and there are enough good race teams that there are 15 cars that hit the setup, and those 15 cars are the ones that finish on the lead lap."

A crew member uses a wire brush to scrape rubber "marbles" off the tires. Marbles are pieces of rubber that come off tires on a race track. When other cars run over them, they stick to the tires.

One of Jeff Gordon's Chevrolet engines at Hendrick Motorsports.

A crew member checks Jeff Gordon's tire pressures before a race.

At most tracks, a car can be adjusted from tight to loose with a change as small as adding or removing one pound of air pressure from one or more tires. That alone can have a major impact on how the car handles. "The revolutionary thing that happened is the radial tire, which you ran on your street car before we ever ran them in Winston Cup racing," Parrot said. "The bias-ply tire would grow. If you had a car that was too tight, what it would do is build the air pressure in the right front tire and it would magnify the problem. But now, with the radial tire, when you go out there, you have a certain amount of stagger built in the tire, and that is exactly what you're going to get. What we do is adjust air pressures and that doesn't adjust the stagger at all, but it adjusts the spring rate of the tire. If we put a pound of air in the right front tire, that means we have put 55 pounds of spring rate on that particular corner of the car, and vice-versa. If we take a pound of air out, then it is 55 pounds of spring rate out of the front. Our race tire—the Goodyear tire—is the optimum tuning tool of every Winston Cup race we go to."

A driver's success boils down to how well he communicates what the car is doing to the crew chief. It can mean the difference between winning and losing a race. A good driver understands the car and relates that knowledge to the crew chief. The best drivers are very effective in describing the handling characteristics of their cars, and highly involved in deciding what adjustments to make. "I don't know where the feeling comes from, if it comes from the seat of the pants, but if you can't feel things before the car starts to do them, then you aren't going to be successful in this business," Martin said. "You have to be able to read the car, just the way you can read one another's language. When you say a word, or two words—a 'little loose'—that could be 1 or 10 pounds

Jimmy Fennig, Mark Martin's crew chief, discusses preparation with one of his crew members at Roush Racing.

of air. Or, 10 pounds of spring or 100 pounds of spring, or 1/16th sway bar or 3/8th sway bar. You and the crew chief have to be able to read one another because the communication means different things to different people. My crew chief, Jimmy Fennig, worked with me in American Speed Association (ASA) for two years, so that helped speed up the process when he came to work for me in Winston Cup. Plus, I have a knack for chassis work. We work in chassis language instead of roundabout talk. We talk about 1/16 and 1/8 and 2,500 pounds. We talk specifics."

"Robin Pemberton is also one of the best at understanding the car's chassis and how to set it up to his liking," said his driver, the fearless Rusty Wallace, who is adept at handling a loose race car.

Pemberton remarked of Wallace's ability, "Rusty is more of a hands-on driver than any other driver I have ever worked with. If the car is not handling right, Rusty overcomes it. I think it is a little bit harder for him to get it better on a tight setup, but I think that is true for everybody. As for Rusty, his setups are closer than probably anybody's when he starts the race. There are very few times where we are way off. We are always within a little bit. I don't think he has a need to adapt as much as others, because I think he starts so much closer than others most of the time."

Rookie Kenny Irwin Jr.'s Texaco/Havoline Ford Thunderbird goes onto the scales and setup pad prior to a practice session. *Photo by Steve Ellis, courtesy of Indianapolis Motor Speedway*

The 1998 season was the first that Wallace and Pemberton worked in a teammate environment. Owner Roger Penske bought part of Michael Kranefuss' Winston Cup team, and the two formed a team operation with driver Jeremy Mayfield. Not only do both drivers exchange ideas, but so do the crew chiefs, Pemberton and Paul Andrews.

Race team engineers provide essential assistance to the crew chiefs. With the sport of NASCAR Winston Cup racing becoming even more competitive, engineers are able to identify ways to find that little extra edge in performance. "As the sport gets more technical, you need a more technical foundation for the team," Pemberton said. "I've been in places before where you had an engineer and you didn't see eye to eye on anything—sunrise or sunset. To make a good marriage out of it, I think it is all a part of getting the engineers to work with the drivers, crew chiefs, and team members."

Ray Evernham at Hendrick Motorsports has some of the best Chevrolet engines for the chassis that he sets up. "I think handling and horsepower are both important," Evernham said. "Right now, the cars are so good, the aerodynamics are so good at certain places, it doesn't take a lot to get a car to handle. You can go to Ronnie Hopkins, get a chassis setup and a chassis and a guy can get close. You can go out and get a guy to put a good

body on a car, and go to a place like Michigan, chassis is not going to override horsepower. But you go to certain tracks like Darlington, you better have handling. At Pocono, handling is critical, but so is horsepower. At some of these places, I'll take the horsepower. Give me some horsepower at Atlanta. At Bristol, it's handling. Texas, newly paved, it could be horsepower. I wouldn't say handling overcomes horsepower everywhere. You would have to be pretty far off. I don't think that at this level, the people we are racing are going to miss it that bad. The guys who are still learning or the guys who are running 10th to 30th, they are going to miss it. But the guys we are racing with, they aren't going to miss it."

Jeff Gordon's crew members check air pressures while the car is in the qualifying line at Bristol Motor Speedway.

Driver Johnny Benson Jr. prepares to put on his helmet before a
qualification attempt at Bristol Motor Speedway.

One of Jeff Gordon's crew members goes over a long prerace
checklist on the DuPont Chevrolet Monte Carlo.

Irvan's crew members use a template to get the rear deck lid of Ernie Irvan's Pontiac back into shape.

Chapter Six

How to Live the NASCAR Lifestyle

No other sport is more demanding than NASCAR Winston Cup racing. With a schedule that begins in early February and ends in mid-November, the teams travel from one end of the country to the other, several times a season. Once the Winston Cup schedule is completed, some teams load up and head to Japan where NASCAR stages an exhibition race at Twin Ring Motegi. When they return, it's off to New York to the NASCAR Winston Cup Banquet in December, then back to the race shop to prepare the cars for the upcoming season. Many teams work through Christmas and New Year's vacations in order to get a car ready for testing at Daytona International Speedway in January. Then, it's back to Daytona Beach, Florida, for Speedweeks and the start of another NASCAR Winston Cup season.

During the racing season, crews get up at 4:30 A.M. on race day and enter the garage at 6 A.M. After a crew performs the grueling job of conducting the race, they have to load up the car and all the equipment to head home. To top it off, there is no such thing as a day off. On Monday morning—the day after a race—they are back in the race shop. "You go in because you have to," explained Ray Evernham. "There is no doubt about it, you get pretty worn out. I'm working seven days a week. On Monday, I try to leave here about 6 P.M., but Tuesday and Wednesday I work 12 or 13 hours. On Thursday, it is back on the road. I'll come in at 6:45 A.M., bring my clothes with me, get on the plane and go to the next race. You would like to develop some kind of way to have a life and do this, too, but I don't know how you can do it at the level we are trying to and still have a life. This has to become your life. Someday you will say, 'I don't want to do it any more.' I'm not going to just half do it and only win half of what we are winning now. I just don't have a private life. My son is seven years old. I've missed a lot of things with him. I don't really see my wife a lot. I have a beautiful house and plenty of toys that I just don't get to play with. I've lived at the lake three years and have been on it less than 10 times. I have two motorcycles with less than

Seven-time NASCAR Winston Cup champion Dale Earnhardt and engine builder Danny Lawrence in the garage area during a break in practice. *Photo by Tim Holle, courtesy of Indianapolis Motor Speedway*

2,000 miles between the two of them. One stretch last year, I was at home, awake, for only eight hours a week."

The biggest foe to a crew chief or mechanic isn't the opposition on the race track, but rather, the fear of getting burned out, both physically and mentally. "I don't think you can avoid it, and I think it happens to everybody," said Evernham. "Anybody who has really accomplished a lot has really put 100 percent into it. I don't know if you can do it any other way. A lot of people can be in this business for a long time and not really give 100 percent and still do okay, but they aren't going to be big winners. Everybody says to me, 'You can't work that hard. You are going to burn yourself out.' Yes, I'm going to burn myself out. I'm probably already burned out. But, we have accomplished a lot."

Evernham does note, however, that burning out may not be all bad. "I would rather give everything I have, then pass right out and be burned out in a short time than have a career that spanned 20 years and say I never gave 100 percent. Phil Jackson (former head coach of the Chicago Bulls of the National Basketball Association) is not going to coach during 1998 because he had had enough. Someday that will happen to me. I've thought and talked about it. There will be a point when that happens."

Evernham keeps his office at Hendrick Motorsports, located near Charlotte Motor Speedway in rural Cabarrus County, North Carolina, and lives in Cornelius, North Carolina, about 35 minutes away. "I get here between 6:30 and 6:45 every morning," Evernham said. "I get up at 5:15, take a shower, stop at the Bagel Bin up at exit 25 on Interstate 77, every morning. That is where I get my direction. Two guys from Long Island opened up a bagel store down here, and they give me a report on how I'm doing and what we need to do for the next week."

Some crew chiefs have even longer drives to and from their shops. When Jimmy Fennig was working at Roush Racing in Liberty, North Carolina, his commute

Crew members repair the damage on Ernie Irvan's Skittles
Pontiac after he backed it into the wall at Bristol Motor Speedway
during practice.

to work every day bordered on being ridiculous. "I lived by Charlotte Motor Speedway and I drove up to Liberty every day," Fennig said. "I would leave at 5 A.M. It was a 1-hour, 45-minute ride one way. The way I looked at it, you don't get an opportunity to work with someone like Mark Martin very often, so the drive every day was well worth it. Mark Martin keeps my energy level up when I watch him drive a race car. He keeps you pumped up, so it doesn't matter how many hours it takes. Now the shop is in Mooresville, and it's closer to my house. I am lucky to have a good, understanding wife and family. You feel bad because you don't get to see your kids grow up. But the time you do get at home, it's precious to me. I'll spend every minute I can with my kids. For instance, I'll drive home after the night race at Bristol, arriving at home at 3 A.M., and then go into the shop from 10 to 12 to reload the truck for a test at Darlington Raceway. I will have been at the track since 7:30 A.M. That's racing."

There is no such thing as free time in racing. Sometimes the mechanics are away from home so long, their dogs growl at them when they get home, wives call the police because a stranger is in the house, and the kids cry because they don't recognize their fathers. Well, not quite, but the crew members are rarely at home. "We don't have any free time," said Todd Parrott, crew chief for Dale Jarrett. "You learn in this sport, it's hard to beat experience. I think I've been fortunate enough that I have gone through just about every situation you could possibly go through. The ups, the downs, the wrecked cars in Happy Hour, blowing motors on race day leading races. You learn how to cope with the good and the bad. I'm very fortunate to have the caliber of people that we have on our race team. Obviously, that takes some pressure off by not having to baby-sit them all the time. You have to have a lot of trust in people. As a crew chief,

New to NASCAR Winston Cup racing is team owner Tim Beverley, who purchased Darrell Waltrip's race team after the three-time Winston Cup champion lost his sponsorship earlier in the 1998 season. *Photo by Tim Ellis, courtesy of Indianapolis Motor Speedway*

A fine example of teamwork, as Irvan's crew all chip in to fix the damaged race car.

if you don't have trust in your guys, it's not going to work. If you tell those guys to change all four of those springs and if you have to stand over them to make sure it is right, then you need to have some different guys. It makes your job easier knowing that you have people who can do the things that you ask them to do."

Parrott knows what it is like to be away from home because when he was growing up, his father, Buddy, a longtime NASCAR crew chief, was rarely at home. "Right now, I have two little boys of my own," said the younger Parrott. "I know what they are going through—growing up as a kid in racing without a father. But I'm trying to make it different than what it was like growing up with my dad being gone all the time. My boys and I get along real well. We are best friends, but we aren't as close as a lot of fathers and sons are. I remember my dad being gone when I was growing up, like playing baseball in high school and him not being there, so my mom would take his place. All the other dads were always there with their kids. It gives you a different outlook on life. I don't want my kids to have to grow up that way."

Crew members who have been in the sport for a long time grow to hate going into the shop on Monday morning after a race. "I'm not a morning person, I like sleeping until the alarm clock has gone off twice," Parrott said. "The morning after a race, I'm worn out. I feel if you have gone through

LEFT: Crew members for Brett Bodine are ready to spring into action when it's time for Bodine's next pit stop in the 1998 Brickyard 400. *Photo by Leigh Spargur, courtesy of Indianapolis Motor Speedway*

RIGHT: Geoff Bodine's pit crew sits and waits for the next pit stop as the laps wind down in the Brickyard 400. *Photo by Tim Ellis, courtesy of Indianapolis Motor Speedway*

a tough race like Indianapolis was for us in 1998, when we came back after running out of gas and making up four laps, I feel like I have cobwebs in my head. I was thinking of everything possible to do to the car to get the laps back, and I was a basket case because my head was so worn out."

Robin Pemberton said no matter how much a crew chief or mechanic tries to balance family with racing, it's nearly impossible. "You think it is going pretty good, then all of a sudden, you have to be away from home an extra week," Pemberton said. "If you didn't want to put up with it, you wouldn't have taken the position when it was offered to you. I enjoy it but there are sacrifices. The thing that bothers most crew chiefs is that their families have to sacrifice as much or more than we do. That is a big problem. You do everything you can to go to all the basketball games and soccer games and baseball games and all that. You try to do the right thing and give the kids the opportunity to go to all the camps they want and take them on vacations or let them travel with you when you can. You try to balance it out by spending that quality time, but it does get quite costly, trying to make up for the fact you aren't there."

A typical work week would be difficult enough for any crew member. But at the end of the week, instead of going home to recover, it's time to head to the race track for more work. "We leave Thursday afternoon between 3 and 5 P.M. I fly on the plane when it is far," commented Pemberton. "Airplanes have saved a lot of it. It would be just miserable without the airplane. We are fortunate enough that Penske takes very good care of us. A few of us are able to fly on Rusty's jet. A lot of Sunday nights, we are home between 7 and 8 P.M. after a race. That is like getting a whole extra day at home.

A race tire serves more than one purpose for this crew member on Joe Nemechek's team. *Photo by Jim Haines, courtesy of Indianapolis Motor Speedway*

Nevertheless, Monday mornings are terrible. On Sundays, you are at work at 6 A.M. By the time the race starts, you have five or six hours in on the job already. Then you have three or four hours of racing, two hours of driving, and a couple hours of flying. You expend a lot of energy on Sunday and it is awfully hard for everybody to show up on Monday and put in a 100-percent effort."

So what is the lure? Why would any mechanic or crew member go through this type of physical and mental fatigue? "There is nothing like racing. It's the competition," Pemberton said. "A lot of people like it. All sports can be exciting, but it's the competition that just happens to be between automobiles that makes it all worth it."

Ray Evernham is so dedicated to his role as crew chief for Jeff Gordon, he averages just eight waking hours at home during any given race week. In fact, this office is probably more familiar than his own home. Nevertheless, he is able to relax by shooting a basketball at a goal installed inside the Hendrick Motorsports race shop.

84   Don Miller, co-owner of Penske Racing South with Roger Penske and Rusty Wallace, stands outside the team's impressive shop. Miller was one of the first team owners to build a shop at Lakeside because the Penske Racing South team wanted to be isolated, away from the hustle and bustle of Charlotte. The only problem was that the rest of the racing community soon followed and built race shops in the park.

Chapter Seven

Mooresville: The Real Hub of NASCAR Winston Cup Racing

When Don Miller and Rusty Wallace were looking for a location to build a race shop in 1989, they were trying to find an out-of-the-way place to get away from the hustle and the bustle of the NASCAR Winston Cup industry in Charlotte, North Carolina. Miller and Wallace, along with Roger Penske, were in the process of forming Penske Racing South, even though Wallace was still in the final year of his contract with team owner Raymond Beadle.

They decided to build in Lakeside Business Park, off Interstate 77 near Mooresville, North Carolina, about 35 miles north of Charlotte. At the time, only Chuck Rider's Bahari Racing team was located there, so Miller, Wallace, and Penske thought they had found their ideal hideaway.

It did not remain a hideaway for long.

Charlotte had long been considered the "hub of NASCAR Winston Cup Racing" but today, the true hub is the Lakeside Business Park. Currently, there are 12 NASCAR Winston Cup and eight NASCAR Busch Series teams headquartered in the industrial park, more than any other single location in the sport. The migration of race teams from Charlotte to Lakeside has turned Mooresville, formerly known as "The Port City," into "Race City, USA." The North Carolina Auto Racing Hall of Fame and Simpson World have also located at Lakeside, along with BSR Racing Parts, Fisher Engineering, Wheels High Performance, Goodridge East Technical Center, Race City Bolt & Nut, Inc., and other racing-related businesses.

Many of the race teams credit Bill Simpson for bringing them to the park. Simpson, a former racer who is responsible for many of the safety innovations in racing today, founded and operates Simpson World at the park, selling racing equipment to the teams and souvenirs to fans. "I'm from Southern California and when I first came here, what I saw was similar to what I saw in the San Fernando Valley from the late 1960s to the early 1970s," Simpson said. "It was basically the same thing—good access to the interstates, good industrial land, and a friendly city government. I knew all the pieces were in place for strong growth. I came in here and bought up a bunch of land and proceeded to sell it all. I sold Ricky Rudd his property for half what the market price was, just so he would come up here. I knew that one would bring another. I sold Penske his property, Dick Moroso his property when he was still in racing, and Michael Kranefuss his property, not with the idea of looking at profit, but with the idea of making something pretty special. And it has turned out to be that way."

Because of Simpson's foresight, Miller and Wallace were only able to enjoy peace and tranquillity for a short period after they moved to Lakeside Business Park in 1990. Like so many others, they purchased property from Simpson. Miller and Wallace were amazed at the tremendous cooperation they received from Mooresville community leaders. "The people in Mooresville were so responsive compared to any place else we had been," Miller said. "We didn't get the typical reaction: 'A race team? Well, that's a dirty word!' The people of Mooresville treated us really nice. I got to know the mayor, the city manager, and some of the other people who were involved. Because they were so responsive, we, too, became a little bit more responsive and started working with the city on some small community projects. The two things started to fall together. Whenever anybody would ask me about how this place was going, I was very positive. Soon, other guys were coming out here, and I unconsciously became the ambassador."

Miller's little secret soon spread throughout the Winston Cup community. Other teams followed them. As new teams were formed, and others wanted to relocate, they all migrated north up Interstate 77. Team owners bought plots of land on speculation while working at shops located elsewhere. It turned out to be a good investment. Penske Racing South bought land for $35,000 to $40,000 an acre in 1989-1990. It is now worth $150,000 an acre. By 1993, the park had become

the prime location for most Winston Cup teams, and now the park is filled to capacity.

Team owner Jack Roush, a recent arrival, has based three of his five teams at Lakeside. He moved Mark Martin from his original shop in Liberty, North Carolina, at the end of the 1997 season. Today, Martin's cars are prepared with Jeff Burton's and Chad Little's in two separate Roush Racing facilities located in the park.

When Ricky Rudd decided to start his own Winston Cup team in 1993, he immediately bought land at Lakeside for his race shop. He temporarily shared space with former team owner D.K. Ulrich in a shop currently occupied by Jasper Motorsports. "When I decided to build a shop, I told myself I'm in this for the long haul," Rudd said. "That first shop was a nice facility, but I wanted to have something of our own. I did this as much as a real estate investment as anything." Careful planning went into the new facility. "The layout was important. We went to all the shops and did a lot of research," Rudd noted. The reaction of the other teams might be regarded by some as "unexpected." People were very friendly, Rudd said without hesitation. "We said, 'Hey, we don't know what we are doing. Give me some ideas, tell me about your shop.' A lot of these shops were these guys' babies. They helped build them. Believe it or not, they would lay it out for you and say, 'This is great, but if you do it this way, you might want to give yourself a few extra feet this way and make changes that way.'" Rudd is quick to add, "I'm not saying we now have the best Winston Cup shop on the circuit, but I'm pretty proud of what we have designed."

Rudd also enlisted the help of his wife, Linda, who served as a business partner when it came to designing the shop and team hauler. "The bottom line was when we decided to do this Winston Cup team, Linda was wanting to build another house before we started anything," Rudd said. "We were so close to building another house, we were able to use all her good ideas putting together a shop instead of a house. She got to do the

LAKESIDE PARK

ROLLINGHILL RD.

Simpson World
United Carolina Bank
Stevens Racing Consultants
Team Simpson Racing
Lakeside Tube Fabricators
Rudd Performance Motorsports
Process Efficiency Products(PEP)
ROE Ltd./Lakeside Park
Butch Mock Motorsports
Penske-Kranefuss Racing
WF Newell & Associates
Hackney & Associates
Concepts

Keller Electric
Mooresville Industrial Supply
Bahari Racing
J-Bear II
Desco, Inc.
Amex Packaging Ltd.
Callaway Service Co.
Downey Products
Athena Building
Fortuna Building
Ultra Motorsports

ROLLINGHILL RD.

RIDGE HILL CIRCLE

KNOB HILL RD.

Ameritech Die & Mold
Plantmasters Inc.
J-Bear I
NC Auto Racing Hall of Fame
Penske Racing
Jasper Motorsports
Jasper Performance Products
Roush Racing

LOMA HILL CIRCLE

MEADOW HILL CR.

Sabco Racing

The directory of the Lakeside Business Park includes some very impressive race teams that operate within the confines of the park. Lakeside is located in Mooresville, North Carolina, at the intersection of Interstate 77 and North Carolina Highway 150.

87

Race-shop tours have become big business at Lakeside, as fans flock to the area to tour the shops and mingle with the teams.

interior decorating on our new hauler instead of laying out a house!"

He has no regrets about the decision to build at Lakeside. "We know just enough about real estate to get into trouble," Rudd said. "We had dabbled in it for a while but kept coming back to the idea of buying in this park. Linda wanted to buy in here for speculation about eight years ago. We ended up waiting four years and paid a higher price to be here. But this park is unique. BSR Racing Products has a parts warehouse in the park so you can practically walk up to the parts house and get what you need. One of the parts vendors comes through the neighborhood like when you were a kid and the Popsicle truck came by. It's a neat concept."

Jack Roush also enjoys the convenience. "As far as advantages, one of the things you don't have to have is a big parts room. Butch Stevens and BSR are right down the street. Instead of UPS overnight or running a truck to Charlotte to get parts, we can get on a golf cart, and in about 45 seconds be in Butch Stevens' parts room, and in another 45 seconds, back at the shop. That has really helped hold the costs down by not having as much inventory."

When Michael Kranefuss left Ford Motor Company as director of Special Vehicle Operations in 1993 to start a NASCAR Winston Cup team, he soon realized the advantages of the park. "It's a good location geographically," said Kranefuss, who originally had

CART FedEx Championship Series team owner Carl Haas as his partner (Haas sold his interest in the team to Penske at the end of the 1997 season). "It's close to Charlotte Motor Speedway and to Interstates 77 and 85. It seemed to be a good investment because a lot of teams were going there. It turned out to be the right decision." Kranefuss is quick to comment that not only was it a good investment to purchase property near Lake Norman, it's nice to be located in a resort area as well. "It's wonderful. You wake up in the morning and you think you are on a vacation," Kranefuss said. "There is nothing there that you wish were different. It's quite convenient."

Kranefuss, like most of the other team owners located in the park, built his shop so fans could stop by to see what goes on in the work area. In the lobby of his building, one of Jeremy Mayfield's show cars is on display, along with free autograph cards and other racing souvenirs for sale. One work bay in the shop is open for the public, to let fans see how Mayfield's Ford Taurus is prepared. "That is a must today," Kranefuss said. "Fans come to see the shop."

Lakeside is not a typical grimy industrial park. It is the showcase of NASCAR racing—a testament to the tremendous growth of the sport. The industrial park has become a tourist destination in Mooresville and the teams and shops are the star attractions. Today, several thousand race fans tour the industrial park each week. As fans from around North America flock to the park to tour the race shops, buy souvenirs, and perhaps get a glimpse of their favorite driver, tour buses have become as common as the fancy race transporters parked along such streets as Raceway Drive and Gasoline Alley. Miller, who thought this could be his hideaway, sometimes has to fight his way through mobs of fans just to go to lunch. "During a week when there are no races in the general vicinity, we get probably 1,500 people who visit the building," said the 60-year-old Miller, who has worked with

Penske for 28 years. "During race weeks though, it's thousands. We don't look at it negatively because without them, we can't do what we do. We try to be as good as we possibly can to them."

The presence of the racing teams has created a self-sufficient community inside the entrance of Lakeside Business Park. Diane Trevisan owns the Winner's Circle Deli. A native of Stuart, Florida, Trevisan is assisted by Amy Daunce of Niagara Falls, New York, and Karen Plyler of Mooresville. The deli is open until 3 P.M., but will accommodate race drivers who want to come in after closing time to avoid the crowds. "We are like the Chamber of Commerce, because everybody wants to know where this is, where that is, where the Hall of Fame is, and stuff like that," Trevisan said. "Rusty came in here on race week; I thought he was crazy, but he did. He got bombarded with fans. Usually he comes in later on in the afternoon when there aren't a lot of people in here. It's like we are all family in here. Everybody knows everybody, and we all take care of each other. If we were across Highway 150, this probably wouldn't do as well."

A few doors down is Race City Bolt & Nut, Inc., owned by Dave Ziegler, who is originally from Canton, Ohio. "The race teams here have really helped my business," Ziegler said. "They are in every day to pick stuff up for the cars. When they need something, they need it now. If you don't have it, they will go down the street. You have to have it for them. I have 110 employees at a place called Ziegler's Bolt & Nut House. I always liked the South, and with my 27 years of experience, this was a 'no-brainer.' It's been real interesting. If they let me have an opportunity to quote them a price, I can blow everybody's price away. So often, the teams had been buying car products and paid 10 times the normal price because they are a race team. Some people gouge race teams like suppliers do on Defense Department contracts. They are doing that to the race teams. But they have done that forever."

The outside of BSR, which stands for Butch Stevens Racing. This is where NASCAR Winston Cup teams come to purchase parts for their race cars.

Denise Francis relocated her Trimmers Hair Salon into the park three years ago. Before that, she was located less than one mile away in Mooresville's biggest shopping center. "It was actually a draw when we selected this place," Francis said. "It's real interesting that even if you weren't a race fan to begin with, you can't help but become one because you are so involved with the people that are in it. We have six people cutting hair, and they average 15 or 20 customers each day, so we run close to 100 people in and out of here. We get a lot of fans who come here looking for race teams, and they see us and stop by for a haircut."

Linda Reese, who is originally from Harrisburg, Pennsylvania, decided to put a fabric shop in the park in 1995. Her friends thought she was crazy putting paisley prints and floral designs in an area known for racing, but it has worked out well. "I'm really glad I put the business here, and the racing industry has helped," Reese said. "A lot of the fans come through race week, and we have the black-and-white checkered racing fabric so we do get some business from the fans. We have a good time when they are in town. We have a lot of women who follow racing who sew and quilt. And we have regular customers as far away as

The Winner's Circle Deli is one of the many non-racing businesses that have prospered by the popularity of the business park and Winston Cup racing. The deli is located inside the industrial park, and its clientele include many NASCAR Winston Cup drivers and crew members.

Canada who are race fans who come in every year to buy fabric from us."

Judy Wallace wanted to be closer to her three boys and grandchildren, so she decided to move to North Carolina. Her three boys are Rusty, Mike, and Kenny Wallace. They drive race cars every weekend. Judy doesn't get much time to see her sons, with one exception. She does see Rusty every day—his picture is all over the inside of the Rusty Wallace Fan Club, which Judy operates in a small office in the park. "We put the fan club here because Rusty's shop is up here," Judy Wallace said. "We moved down here three years ago. I was still running the fan club up in Missouri. We wanted a fan club that was convenient. Lucky enough, this was the last slot they had in the unit. There have been a lot of people walking in—large groups, bus tours, everything comes through here now. We have never really pushed this fan club, mainly for selfish reasons because I'm as busy as I want to be. We never think there are too many people who come through the park, though. We're used to dealing with crowds at the race tracks. Most of them are in a friendly mood, and it is fun to talk to them."

Outside Lakeside Business Park, the teams' presence has also created a booming business environment. Hotels, motels, and restaurants are being built in the area around the park off Exit 36 on Interstate 77. "I think this park is the whole reason why all the new hotels, motels, and restaurants in the area are being opened," Miller remarked. "This whole area is expanding from a commerce standpoint, basically because of what the racing industry has brought here: more homes, more children, educational needs, and more spending. Business around here is booming. That is what that community thrives on—that's what drives it."

Despite all of the convenience, there are downsides. "The drawback to this," Rudd said, "is if any of your guys become unhappy, they don't even need a truck to move their tool boxes. They can just grease up the wheels and move it down the street." That has actually happened. "It hasn't happened with people moving out, but we have had some people move in over lunch," Roush added. "Secrets getting exchanged over beers was a fear of mine, but with the guys we have involved in our program right now, there certainly hasn't been a manifestation of any kind of a problem with information being disseminated carelessly."

Simpson, the man with the vision to create what has become the hub of NASCAR Winston Cup Racing concluded, "The people here are pretty cooperative. It's pretty refreshing when you deal with a city and they want to work with you. Most of the places I've been, you will go to a city with an idea and they don't want to talk with you. But Mooresville has been very good. You couldn't ask for a better group of people to work with. They see this place expanding. I'm looking at it and say this is just the tip of the iceberg. There will be more expansion beyond this."

There may come a day, however, when the Lakeside Business Park becomes too congested for some of the more secretive race teams. For now, however, the park has all the advantages a race team could want. "I don't think there is anyone in the park who doesn't appreciate what they have," Miller said. "I believe everyone who is here has made a tremendous investment. It would be a pretty tall order to find something better."

Judy Wallace is as proud as a mother can be of her three sons, race drivers Rusty Wallace, Kenny Wallace, and Mike Wallace. Judy runs the Rusty Wallace Fan Club from an office at the Lakeside Business Park.

NASCAR Winston Cup driver Dale Jarrett is in the lime-green car, ahead of Jeff Gordon in the white No. 3, Tony Stewart in No. 7, eventual race winner Mark Martin in the aqua car. *Photo by Steve Snoddy, courtesy of Indianapolis Motor Speedway*

Chapter Eight

Saturday Night Racing, IROC Style

Imagine what it would be like to remove the variables of a team, car, or engine advantage from auto racing and then make it a battle of 'May the best driver win.'" That is what Roger Penske and Les Richter envisioned 25 years ago when they created the International Race of Champions series (IROC). Their concept was to put 12 of the world's best race drivers in identically prepared race cars so that driving skill, rather than a horsepower or aerodynamic advantage, would be showcased. The legendary battles in IROC history are testaments to the driver's skill, more so than one particular car having a major advantage over another.

Racing fans are a unique breed who are very loyal to their favorite drivers. But sometimes the drivers are unable to show their true skills if they are hampered by an equipment disadvantage. Fans who come out to watch a race, however, are rooting for a driver more than a specific make of car. In essence, IROC is a great showcase for driver ability. "That's the idea," said Mark Martin, a four-time IROC champion who is second in all-time career wins in

the series with eight. In Winston Cup racing, Martin and his Roush Racing team often have superior equipment to complement Martin's outstanding driving ability. But when the competition is equal, Martin really shines behind the wheel. "Equal cars have been sweet to me," Martin said. "I've had a lot of frustrations over the years in racing with fuel mileage and pit stops that have broken my heart in races that I thought we were going to win. But to go out there now, I don't have to worry about somebody having more motor or a better chassis setup—I just go out there and race."

"It's an old adage of a fan saying, 'If I had a car just like Jeff Gordon, I bet I would blow his doors off,'" said Jay Signore, president of IROC. "That is where the concept came from—why don't we take Dale Earnhardt's team and Jeff Gordon's team and take that advantage away from the driver and give him a car that is already set up? They wouldn't have a say in how it is set up because you would have your test drivers do it, thereby equalizing the drivers. Then you would see who the best driver is."

Mechanics check tire pressures and work on the setup of an IROC car during testing at the Indianapolis Motor Speedway. *Photo by Jim Haines, courtesy of Indianapolis Motor Speedway*

Roger Penske is best known for outstanding innovation in Indy car racing. The former driver-turned-team-owner is the all-time victory leader in the Indianapolis 500 with 10 victories and is known for leading the way in cutting-edge racing technology in the CART. He is the driving force behind Penske Speedways and he understands the value of close competition.

"It is hard to look ahead 25 years but what we have tried to do is do it a year at a time, and so far, it has been outstanding," Penske said. "Overall, we have established the credibility with the drivers that we build good, safe cars. You've seen people start in the back and come to the front. To me, from the standpoint of having equal cars, are they always perfect? They probably never are.

But the key thing is we keep getting great drivers to run in the series."

Although today's IROC series features 12 identically prepared Pontiac Firebird Trans Am cars, the original IROC, in 1973, had Porsche Carrera RSR cars in a series contested entirely on road courses. Emerson Fittipaldi, the Formula One champion at that time, was the fastest qualifier for the first-ever IROC race at Riverside, California. Signore was part of the series from its genesis. "I've been involved in the floor operation since 1973," Signore said. "The first IROC was Porsches, but those were built in Germany and came over in a boat ready to race. We had technicians from the factory working along with us. We did some minor work on them. All that took place as a factory-supported effort, 100 percent. In 1974, we built Camaros, much like the current Trans Am car was in the 1970s. That was really a modified street car. In 1976, we went to Banjo Matthews and got our first Banjo chassis. From 1976 through 1984, we ran Banjo-style racing cars, which was basically a Busch Grand National style of car."

Today's IROC series features cars built by South Carolina chassis builder Mike Laughlin, with a steel tube chassis similar to a Winston Cup car. The cars are then shipped to IROC headquarters in Tinton Falls, New Jersey, where Signore's crew of 22 mechanics does the rest of the work. "I think we have made a lot of improvements, but a lot of that is like any racer, no matter what he runs or what series he runs in, is paying attention to the most minute detail," Signore said. "You start from the bottom up and don't let any dimension or any number run away from you. Those are the things that keep the cars getting better and better and better. That is where the equalization part comes in. We use a spec engine. Everything in our car is done 'according to spec'—meaning that when building a car, everything is identical to the specs to keep them equal and reliable. Those are the controls. If you can't control the package 100 percent, then the next best thing you can do is spec the gear, spec the tires, spec the compression ratio, spec the carburetor. Those things help control and keep things on an even parity.

"There is performance enhancement through shock absorbers. In the current cars, that is what you are hearing. In Winston Cup, they change the shock to make the car handle better. With the advent of the Penske shock, you can take it apart and build it and tune it to your own specifications. One important asset that we have is a shock dyno. Buying a shock and taking it apart and putting it back together again is pretty easy, but knowing exactly what you are doing is the hard part. That is where the dyno is a necessity. Even though you develop parity with a shock absorber, you add a little cost with the dynamometer. But when you are building all the cars to be equal, that is probably one of the major things we have done."

Ninety-two of the greatest names from around the world have competed in IROC since 1973. But does the series really prove who is the best driver? "We don't know if IROC determines who the best driver in the world is, but we sure go a long way toward that goal," said Richter, IROC's chairman. "IROC does prove that some drivers have more skill than others regardless of their racing background."

Saturday Night short track racing has moved closer

Setting up the cars equally for the 12 drivers that participate in IROC is a difficult task. That is why the three test drivers of IROC—Jim Sauter, Dick Trickle, and Dave Marcis—have an important job in giving feedback to the IROC mechanics. *Photo by Jim Haines, courtesy of Indianapolis Motor Speedway*

IROC president Jay Signore is the man in charge of the racing series that brings 12 of the world's best drivers together for the four-race series. *Photo by Jim Haines, courtesy of Indianapolis Motor Speedway*

to standardized racing in similar equipment. IROC epitomizes that philosophy. And yet, even though the concept behind the IROC series is similar to many Saturday night race tracks, Signore's high-tech shop is remarkably similar to many of the top Winston Cup shops on the circuit. "It's pretty expensive," Signore admits. "We all pretty much know what a stock car costs. Our cars are a little bit cheaper than a Winston Cup car, primarily because we don't dump cubic dollars into our engines. We have the best parts in our engines, such as Carillo rods, and good crankshafts with Chevrolet-machined blocks and top-notch heads. There is nothing cheap in

our cars. The budget to run it, including a lot of travel and testing expense, runs upward of $4 million a year. We have 22 employees on a day-to-day basis and we bring in another five or six guys who have been working for us for years who help us at the race tracks."

Working for IROC has given many mechanics tremendous hands-on experiences. According to Signore, "If a guy has some basic skills and some interest in racing, the way we run our operation helps further his career," Signore said. "It takes us about six weeks to roll the cars over, pull the engines and do what we have to do to them. We build all of our engines in-house. We have four guys in our body shop, we have three guys in our fabrication shop, two guys in our parts area and whoever is left out of that number is working on the main floor. We have approximately six guys on the floor doing the maintenance work, and we also have a fellow who does our unit repairs, and that is the rear ends and the transmissions."

"We pay attention to detail in the shop. For example, when we get a surface-plate chassis from Mike Laughlin, that car comes up to our shop and we mount it on our own surface plate. Anything we need to attach to that chassis gets done on that surface plate. This allows us to make our cars more compatible and the parts more interchangeable. All of our body panels are done the same way. We actually do a full-scale model in clay, which is fairly expensive. Then we do our molds. Every hole that is drilled in the body is prescheduled and premarked, so when we get a body panel from our fiberglass house, it is already drilled. We have templates to qualify it. Then we drill all those pieces together. Finally, that body can actually go to the paint shop, be painted separately, and then it is ready to bolt on any car."

A quick look at IROC's list of champions proves the wisdom of the strategy. Mark Donohue, Bobby Unser, A.J. Foyt, Al Unser, Mario Andretti, Bobby Allison, Cale Yarborough, Harry Gant, Al Unser Jr., Geoff Bodine,

An IROC Pontiac Trans Am being prepared in the garage area. *Photo by Jim Haines, courtesy of Indianapolis Motor Speedway*

Terry Labonte, Dale Earnhardt, Rusty Wallace, Ricky Rudd, Davey Allison, and Mark Martin all have won the IROC title.

IROC is about great drivers in equally prepared cars. Nevertheless, it has also brought some outstanding mechanics into the sport, most notably Ray Evernham, crew chief for two-time NASCAR Winston Cup champion Jeff Gordon. "I'm proud of Ray and hopefully, IROC had a little to do with his success at Hendrick Motorsports," Signore said. "Ray is a unique person: he is driven and he works hard at what he is doing. Ray really has attention for detail. He came to our place and worked hard, put in a lot of hours and effort. You see that continuing. A guy who works with that much energy deserves to be where he is. He didn't get there

because he sat on his tush or somebody gave him a hand. Ray works hard at what he does."

Signore concluded by saying, "Ray is a psychologist and a pretty decent technician. He was also a pretty good short track driver up in New Jersey. That is a great combination." Signore recounted one particular event that supports his contention, "When a driver came in to Ray and explained to him the car was loose, Ray had some sense of what the driver was talking about. Nine-tenths of our battle in racing today is managing people and getting everybody to work together and have both oars in the water and pulling for the team. There is not a single soul who can do it himself, not me, or Roger Penske, or Ray Evernham, or anybody else. It's putting a good team together, recognizing that team or being able

CART FedEx Championship Series driver Jimmy Vasser, in the gold
car, leads the 12-car starting field to the green flag to start the
first-ever IROC race at the Indianapolis Motor Speedway. *Photo by
Bill Watson, courtesy of Indianapolis Motor Speedway*

The field goes through the first turn at the Indianapolis Motor Speedway. That's seven-time NASCAR Winston Cup champion Dale Earnhardt in the blue car. *Photo by Ron McQueeny, courtesy of Indianapolis Motor Speedway*

to manage a team. Everybody works together and works for a common goal. It's not an 'I', it's a 'we.'"

Ironically, Evernham himself was a Saturday night racer and has helped popularize IROC's standardized racing formula, which is used at many Saturday night tracks today. "It showcases the driver more than the car, but you have to remember on Saturday night, you can change your springs and shocks and stagger your tires and change your pressure and move weight around," Evernham said. "In IROC, you can't do that. In IROC, the cars truly are equal. Those cars are way more equal than people ever give them credit for. I think sometimes it is Jay's worst enemy. He works so hard to get the cars equal that it doesn't make for a good show sometimes."

Evernham admits it takes a different train of thought to set cars up equally, because mechanics are normally trained to make one car go faster than another. "It helps you to work to exact specifications because every car has to be exact," Evernham said. "Camber, caster, height, weight—everything has to be exact. It makes you be a lot more precise, even when you are doing a one-off car, because you are trained that way. If it calls for 2 degrees of caster, it gets 2 degrees of caster—not 1/4. To find an optimum setup, we would go and test, do a lot of testing and use three or four different test drivers. They would decide the optimum setup. Then, we would go through, take the test car, do a blueprint off that test car and match all the other cars to it."

Today's test drivers in IROC include NASCAR Winston Cup drivers Dave Marcis and Dick Trickle as well as veteran short track racer Jim Sauter. "When I started there, it was actually George Follmer, Dave

A two-by-two traffic jam at high speed down the front stretch of
the Indianapolis Motor Speedway. *Photo by Harlen Hunter, courtesy of
Indianapolis Motor Speedway*

Marcis, and me," Evernham recalled. "I was actually a test driver. That is one of the reasons I went there. It has to be a combination between the drivers and the stopwatch. They tried not to set a car up in one particular driver's favor. At that time, we had George Follmer, who was a road racer, and we tried to use him to get a feel for what the Formula One guys would want. Dave was a stock car racer, so if you set the car up the way Dave wanted it, you probably couldn't get a Derek Bell or a Jackie Ickx or somebody like that comfortable. So you had to take a guy like George Follmer, who wasn't necessarily a stock car racer, and let him get a feel for it.

"The cars have gotten even closer than when I was there. It has been 10 years since I've been there and they have made great strides," Evernham noted. "They have evolved no differently than NASCAR Winston Cup racing has evolved. They do a tremendous job over there. I can see where they are working in areas we talked about and thought about but just didn't have the technology to do. They have a lot more tools now to keep the cars equal."

When it comes to the Saturday night short tracks, however, Signore—the father of standardized racing—does not want to see the local racer lose sight of looking

Safety workers survey the damage on Jeff Burton's car after a fourth-lap crash involving Arie Luyendyk and Tommy Kendall brought out the red flag at Indianapolis. *Photo by Kay Nichols, courtesy of Indianapolis Motor Speedway*

Here is an example of a gamble that failed. Dale Jarrett's crew pushes the Ford Quality Care Ford Taurus back to its pit area after it ran out of fuel while leading at the midway point of the 1998 Brickyard 400. Jarrett had dominated the race up to that point, and the mistake may have cost him over $1 million. *Photo by Jim Haines, courtesy of Indianapolis Motor Speedway*

Chapter Nine

Gambles That Work, and Some That Don't

Gambling is as much a part of auto racing as pits stops, flat tires, and crashes. A crew chief often has to think like a high-stakes poker player in Las Vegas if his team is going to go to victory lane. For Dale Jarrett, the 1998 Brickyard 400 became that type of race, at the midway point of the season.

The Indianapolis Motor Speedway has a way of magnifying mistakes by a race driver or team into gaffes of monumental proportions. The Indianapolis 500 is filled with tales of drivers who took a gamble, made the wrong decision, and lost a chance at victory.

It's very easy to go from hero to goat at the 2.5-mile Speedway. Dale Jarrett and his Robert Yates Racing team discovered that in the fifth Brickyard 400. With 200 miles to go, Jarrett was in the lead and running away with the race. He was preparing to come in for a pit stop on the 81st lap, when his Ford Taurus ran out of fuel on the backstretch. Jarrett coasted with the car around the race track, but it only went as far as the entrance to pit road. Unfortunately,

Jarrett's pit stall was at the opposite end, so his crew had to run the length of the pits then push the stalled car to the pit area. By the time Jarrett's car was refueled, he was four laps down. Amazingly, Jarrett was able to make up all four laps. He finished the race on the lead lap, in 16th place.

After the race, it was obvious Jarrett was furious with his crew chief, Todd Parrott. "We ran out of gas," Jarrett said. "We had a great race car. I drove the race car. I came in when they told me to come in and that is all that I did. We simply ran out of gas, even though we had a super race car." Parrott had little more to say about the mistake.

Team owner Robert Yates had more to say on the subject that kept Jarrett from becoming the first two-time winner of the Brickyard 400. "If the guys that worked on that car are smart enough to get a car that good, then they're certainly smart enough to figure out not to let that happen again," Yates explained. "Nothing had to be said on Monday morning. Their hearts were eating at them, and they knew they would have it fixed next time."

One of Dale Jarrett's crew members contemplates the gamble that didn't pay off after Jarrett returns to the Brickyard 400. *Photo by Tim Holle, courtesy of Indianapolis Motor Speedway*

Jack Roush, team owner for NASCAR Winston Cup drivers Mark Martin, Jeff Burton, Johnny Benson Jr., Chad Little, and Kevin Lepage, is one of the best in the business when it comes to carburetion and getting the most mileage out of a tank of fuel. *Photo by Jim Haines, courtesy of Indianapolis Motor Speedway*

In this situation, few would fault Yates had he gone to the race shop Monday morning and reprimanded his crew. But his is a different approach. "I'm not playing in any of those guys shoes," Yates said. "They've won a lot of races, and I'm sure they are kicking themselves a hell of a lot more than I could kick them Monday morning. Actually, I won't kick them at all. I'm going to pat them on the back and try to see what they need the next time. Today, we certainly felt like we could beat Jeff Gordon (who won the race)."

Disappointed, yes, but not frustrated. Yates would rather run up front than never make it there in the first place. "The most frustrating part of racing is when you can't figure out how to run up front," Yates said. "It can get so far out in left field and that's when it's frustrating. We just wish they would schedule another one tomorrow." A few days after the 400, Parrott was able to reflect on the error that kept Jarrett from winning the race. "I was over it the next day," said Parrott, who called the shots when Jarrett won the Brickyard 400 in 1996. "It tears at you, knowing we had a shot at winning that much money and being the first two-time winner of the Brickyard 400. If I think about it, we should have won the last three Brickyard 400s."

Parrott, like many crew chiefs in NASCAR Winston Cup racing, never went to college. But he and others who never went past high school know more about the race car than many college-educated engineers. "When I got out of high school I decided I wanted to be a crew chief," Parrott said. "I didn't go to college, I went to the University of NASCAR. We may not have gone to college, but sometimes we know more than the engineers who are sent down here. It is hard to beat experience. There are no dummies out here. I've been fortunate enough to have the best teachers in racing—Harold Elliott, Barry Dodson, Jimmy Makar, Robin Pemberton, Larry McReynolds, and Rusty Wallace. And my dad, too. I learned how to work with people and call shots in the pits during the race more from my dad than anyone else."

Robin Pemberton, like so many others, owes much of his success to taking a gamble. The biggest chance Pemberton ever took did not come on the race track, but it did affect his career. "My biggest gamble was moving from New York to here," Pemberton said. "I don't think there are any good gambles that have worked or done any great things for us. One remembers the gambles that failed more than the ones that worked." As an example, Pemberton recalls, "We took on two tires at Charlotte in the Coca-Cola 600, and Jeff Gordon is a fifth- or sixth-place car, and he takes on four. He didn't have to fight anyone to get to us and pass us, and we finished second. That was a big gamble that didn't work."

In spite of ventures like this, Pemberton admits, "I'm not a big gambler. I'm pretty conservative when it comes to everything. We haven't done too well with our two-tire versus four-tire strategy at any time. It's important for us to have a car that is good enough to where you don't have to gamble during a race. We fool with air pressures and that basically comes from Rusty. He is so sensitive to all of that, he can pick it apart and he knows exactly what he needs with tire pressure. There is no time we have been at odds over tire pressure."

By taking a conservative approach, Pemberton is able to lead by example. He values communication over a gamble that may not work. "You have to be able to communicate, you have to be willing to do that," Pemberton said. "It's the same problem everybody goes through, you can only lead by example so much. You have to set the standard or set the example. To get the respect of the people, you have to get in there and gouge with them and do everything they are willing to do. There are a lot of different examples. Some guys hit it off right off the bat and you have to be able to maintain that. Very few relationships last over a few years professionally. Drivers and crew chiefs have learned that you have to be able to head trouble off at the pass long before it starts. You have to maintain a good relationship with the driver and all the crew members."

Crew chief Larry McReynolds and crew member David Smith plot race strategy for driver Mike Skinner. By gambling on fuel at Watkins Glen, Skinner was rewarded with the highest finish of his career when he came home third. *Photo by Tim Holle, courtesy of Indianapolis Motor Speedway*

The circumstances that lead to taking a gamble are often dictated by the events of each race. "You have to be able to think on your feet," Pemberton said. "So many things happen, you have to make a split-second decision as the car comes down pit road. You have to have a strategy or plan laid out, but that is only to set parameters. You have to adjust it during the race."

Gambles come in many different ways, but two in particular are the most popular: stretching fuel mileage and changing two tires rather than four. More often than not, however, gambles can backfire. "There are all kinds of gambles you take on different chassis setups," Ernie Irvan said. "After Happy Hour, you might make some radical changes. There have been some times we have done that. A driver can't be afraid to gamble and the crew chief can't, either."

Jack Roush, team owner for Mark Martin, Jeff Burton, Johnny Benson Jr., Chad Little and Kevin Lepage, is a master at tuning the carburetor just right so his dri-

One of Jimmy Spencer's crew members thinks of gambling during the 1998 Brickyard 400, atop his perch on the team's toolbox. *Photo by Leigh Spargur, courtesy of Indianapolis Motor Speedway*

vers get the very best fuel mileage. "He won us Dover with fuel mileage," said Jimmy Fennig, Martin's crew chief. "Jack is a good person and he understands racing. He understands if you are having a bad day, and what to do to fix it the next time. One thing about Jack, if he has a problem, he will work on it until he fixes it."

During the 1998 season, Jeff Gordon was on the winning end of most of Ray Evernham's gambles, but there were a few that did not work, such as when he ran out of fuel at Dover in June. But the payoffs to Evernham's gambles are often very big, especially when they allow Gordon to drive into victory lane. Although Gordon felt that 1998 was "our year to win one" at Michigan Speedway, he admitted that his victory in the Pepsi 400 there in August was the result of a risky gamble. "The only reason we won was luck," Gordon said. "Some cars," he said, "had handled 'just right' after taking on four tires on a pit stop. But when they put two tires on, their cars got real tight. My car was real loose but when I put two tires on, it was perfect. It was exactly what I needed to run 17 or 20 laps. It's just circumstances, how things work out there. Had we put on four tires, I would have still been loose and those guys would have driven away from us. I make sure Ray gets a lot of credit because he deserves it," Gordon said. "At that time, I really didn't think two tires was the right call, but I didn't question him. I kept my mouth shut, and said I was going to drive that thing as hard as I could." Evernham's reply was simple, "Tighten those belts up, stand up in that seat because you're going to have to drive this thing. You only have two tires." The gamble turned out right; the car was perfect on two tires. Gordon's take on the gamble that he felt wouldn't work, "That is what makes us such a great combination. It is hard to find that type of relationship and confidence that goes back and forth."

Mark Martin comes in for a pit stop during the 1998 Brickyard 400. Martin finished second to race winner Jeff Gordon. Teams often gamble in the pits when they decide to change either two or four tires during a pit stop. *Photo by Dave Edelstein, courtesy of Indianapolis Motor Speedway*

A closer look at the dashboard of Wallace's race car shows the order of the gauges on the dash.

Chapter Ten

The View from the Driver's Seat

Almost everyone remembers their driver's education classes. It all seemed very simple. The instructor first told you to adjust the seat, hook on the seat belt, and adjust the rearview and sideview mirrors. The preparation before the key was ever turned, that is what the instructor reminded you was the most important part of driving.

Try to imagine what it is like to climb through the window of a NASCAR Winston Cup car, into a seat so tight it makes John Glenn's cockpit in his 1962 Mercury spacecraft seem roomy. A Winston Cup car is built for performance, not luxury. Instead of the aesthetically pleasing array of instruments found on the driver's dash in a passenger car, the Winston Cup car's interior is sterile. Don't look for a fancy clock or speedometer on this dashboard—the most important instruments are the tachometer and the oil temperature, water temperature, and oil pressure gauges.

Forget about adjusting the seat in a Winston Cup car. It's molded to fit the driver's body and bolted to the floorboard of the chassis. The seat leaves little room for the body to move. This is actually a safety feature to prevent injury in a crash. Other safety features are incorporated where luxury normally took precedence. Instead of a fold-down armrest and a console to his or her right, the NASCAR driver sits next to a thick cross-member—a metal post that keeps the roof from collapsing during a crash. The right-side window cannot be rolled up or down; it's Plexiglas, which, in addition to not shattering like stock window glass, helps the aerodynamics of the car. In the driver's window, netting keeps the driver's head and arms inside the car in case of a crash. In the days before window netting, a driver's head could hit the wall if the driver's side hit first. A fire extinguisher is situated on the console near the seat, so it is accessible from both windows of the car. If a driver is unconscious, a safety worker can reach in and set it off. Comfort is far from a priority in a Winston Cup car. There is no AM/FM stereo radio, but there is a two-way radio used for crew-driver communication.

The inside of Rusty Wallace's Ford Taurus shows this is not a car built for comfort.

Each gauge on the driver's dash serves a specific purpose, giving him important information that can be relayed to the crew. "The dash has specific dimensions spelled out in the rule book," said Preston Miller, NASCAR Winston Cup project manager for the Ford Motor Company. According to Miller, the dash is a certain distance back from the base of the windshield internally and the face must be a minimum height of six inches. There are structural members just behind the dash that are integral parts of the roll cage.

NASCAR requires analog gauges. But the arrangement of the dials on the dash can vary from one driver to the next. "The gauges are all in the dash in a designated location," Miller said. "The way the gauges are oriented, which way the needles point, is critical. A lot of times the driver will twist the gauge where the needles all point in one direction, usually straight up,

regardless of whether it is oriented correctly for that particular gauge or not. That way, they don't look to read; they look for position of the needles. If, in a glance, one needle is not pointing up, you take a second look at it."

In the important function of monitoring the gauges and transmitting the data back to the pits, many different styles have evolved. "Everybody has his own particular format," Ricky Rudd said. "They have a certain place they want to look at the oil pressure, a place they want to look at the tachometer. Every driver is different with the placement of the gauges. Throughout my career, I have had an arrangement in which I place my gauges so that I don't have to look all over the place for an oil pressure gauge. I know where it is. So whatever car I drive, I put it in that position. It's all driver preference. Usually, the tach is right in the center, with the oil gauges all together.

"I would prefer to have the voltmeter all the way to the right, but the way our dash panel is laid out, we have it as a module," Rudd continued. "We can take those four buttons out and the whole electrical panel will unhook for quick replacement. But the big gauges I look at are the water temperature, the oil pressure, and oil temperature. The oil temperature is real important at a track like Daytona, because if it is not up to temperature when you make a qualifying run, it will slow you down about 1 mile per hour. If you don't monitor it during the race, it will get too hot and melt your motor down. That is pretty important at Daytona, because you run as much tape on the grille as you possibly can stand, so you really have to watch your temperature gauges."

Rusty Wallace likes to have his gauges placed in order of importance, so that when he is traveling at speeds approaching 200 miles per hour, he can take a quick glance to check them. "The least important gauge in the car is the amp gauge," Wallace explained. "I'm always paying attention to the tachometer on the restarts, so I have to have it in good sight. The next important gauge is the water temperature. The third most important is the oil temperature, and the fourth most important is the oil pressure. A lot of people think that's the most important because if you lose oil pressure, you are out of the race. But if you have an oil pressure problem, you are out anyway. I try to position it so I can glance down on restarts and see them. I don't have to look around the steering wheel and see different things. I try to put my mirrors in a position where I'm

Note the arrangement of the pedals near the floorboard of Rusty Wallace's Ford Taurus.

An even more detailed look at Wallace's dashboard shows six toggle switches that are used for various aspects of the car.

not obstructed. Some drivers put mirrors real close to them, others put their mirrors way far away from them. Every driver has his own different style. My style is to position everything to how it ranks."

In Wallace's Miller Lite Ford Taurus, from left to right, are the tachometer, the water temperature, oil temperature, oil pressure, and amp meter gauges. To the left of the gauges are switches. One controls the ignition that puts power to the ignition box, another does nothing but spin the starter over to start firing the engine. There is also a helmet switch, which blows air into the helmet, an air conditioning switch for the cool suit, and other switches that operate fans and brake coolers.

The cockpit of Rudd's Tide Ford Taurus is set up much the same way as Wallace's car. "We have a fan switch that runs the electric motor on the back of the radiator, much like a street car has on it today, but we control it from the cockpit," Rudd said. "The helmet switch is the blower fan that runs to the driver's helmet. The brake switch is a brake blower that works the brake blower motors on the short tracks. We don't have that on a superspeedway car. The red knob by the oil gauges is the brake bias, which changes from front to rear brake bias on the car. It changes whether you want front brake or rear brake. You don't really fool with it too much on a superspeedway or intermediate speedway; it is more a short track or road course thing. We have an ignition key on the crossbar that turns the main battery switch off. The fire extinguisher and the master cutoff switch are on the dash."

A look at the seat Wallace sits in during a race. These seats are the latest design for driver safety.

On the left side of the driver's seat is a mandatory leg brace that all Winston Cup drivers must have installed in their cars. With so many crossbars and leg braces, it's a very tight fit in the cockpit of the race car. The seat itself has very little padding and is rigid so the driver feels what the car is actually doing. "You hear the term, 'Drive by the seat of your pants,' but the more you can feel the car, the more you are in touch with the car . . . the better you can feel if the race car is loose, if it is pushing or whatever," Rudd said.

Behind the driver's seat is an array of ducts and blowers and condensers, all with specific functions. Unlike a passenger car, which has sideview mirrors on both sides, a NASCAR Winston Cup machine has none. This is for both safety and aerodynamic reasons. In crashes, mirrors could fly into the driver's compartment, injuring the driver, or they could land on the race course, creating one more piece of hazardous debris. That means the driver has to be very careful, use the rearview mirror inside the race car, and listen

117

One of Jeff Gordon's Chevrolet Monte Carlos, minus the paint job.

to his spotter, who is usually on a spotter's stand atop a grandstand.

"When I do my scan out the window and in the rearview mirror, if I can't see anybody, I have to assume there isn't anybody there, although what helps me is the spotter," Wallace explained. "The blind spot in my car is my left-rear corner. If you are passing a guy, you know you have passed him, and he is back there somewhere, so you try to give him a little extra room. On the straight-

aways, you can see a guy take a duck to the inside, and you know where he is at all the time. You have to be aware—you can't totally rely on your spotter. You have to do a lot of things on your own. A lot of that comes from driving race cars for so long and having a lot of experience at it."

Like most drivers in the NASCAR Winston Cup, Wallace uses a full-face helmet. He began his career using an open-face helmet, which gave him better vision

Kyle Petty's crew work on the Hot Wheels Pontiac.

Jeff Gordon's Chevrolet Monte Carlo being pushed to the front of
the qualification line.

but not as much protection to his head and face. "It took me a good while to get used to, because it felt like it was always confining, like it was closing up my peripheral vision," Wallace said. "That is one reason why I got Bill Simpson to make the openings wider in my helmet, to bring them back farther. Since then, he has done that to a lot of people's helmets. Now, when I take the full-face helmet off and put an open-face on, I feel real weird."

Despite all the preparation that goes into a race car, parts often fail, including the gauges. When the gauges work, however, they give the driver and the team an indication when something is about to go wrong. "The oil temperature is the first indicator of having a problem," said Robin Pemberton, Wallace's crew chief. "Then, you look down and see the pressure and make sure you have the same oil pressure you have been running, whether it is 50 pounds or 100 pounds. Then, you watch your water temp. When an engine gets ready to blow, generally the driver feels it first. If it is going to blow, they feel it shaking or smell something first and that will alert them to look at the gauges. Your oil temperature, water temperature, and oil pressure gauges, you will notice first. But when the rear end goes, there is no gauge that will tell the driver."

Despite all the gauges and switches that play key roles in the race car's performance, the driver is usually not in the best position to know what is really going on during a race. "The television audience knows more about what is going on in these races than the driver does or the crew members," Miller said. "The audience has the benefit of looking at things the driver can't see."

One of Ricky Rudd's crew members works on the front airdam of the Tide Ford Taurus. Teams like to run the cars as low to the track as possible, but the cars must meet NASCAR technical specifications.

Members of Geoff Bodine's pit crew kick back in a rare moment of relaxation during the long, hard NASCAR Winston Cup season. *Photo by Kay Nichols, courtesy of Indianapolis Motor Speedway*

The NAPA 500 at Atlanta Motor Speedway in November is the showcase event at a showplace facility. It is the race that typifies what NASCAR Winston Cup racing is all about. It is what the entire season comes down to. This is what all the hard work by the race teams, the countless hours of preparation and testing, and the long, hot, grueling hours behind the wheel of a race car lead up to—the final race of the NASCAR Winston Cup season, the race that often determines the championship.

For the teams not involved in the battle for the Winston Cup, it represents one last opportunity to win a race and gain much-needed momentum for the following season. For those teams that are in the Winston Cup title chase, it's one final weekend of intense pressure that reaches its culmination in 500 miles of high-speed racing at the 1.54-mile speedway.

Mention the name of the race and the speedway to Ray Evernham, and he gets nervous. Gordon clinched the 1995 and 1997 championships at Atlanta, but saw his hopes of winning a title in 1996

end as his Hendrick Motorsports teammate, Terry Labonte, came through in the clutch. In all three season-finales during that span, Gordon has been less than spectacular. Evernham will be the first to admit that. "That is one of the biggest-pressure races of the year and we run awful at Atlanta," Evernham said. "Our last tests are going to be used up at Atlanta. We have one win there, and we have just been awful. Again, that is another track we are studying. We are going to go there and somehow, some way, run better." Gordon has won at Atlanta, but he won in 1995, when the track was still in its original oval configuration. Bruton Smith, chairman of the board of Speedway Motorsports, Inc., decided to flip-flop the frontstretch with the backstretch and reconfigure the facility into a quad-oval concept, making it similar to his tracks in Charlotte and Fort Worth, Texas.

"We were awful in November, and we were awful in March," Evernham said of the first two races run on the new quad-oval race course in 1997 and 1998. "I have to get a handle on the place. Everybody else runs well there, but I don't think anybody else is real

Todd Parrott, Dale Jarrett's crew chief, plots race strategy in his office inside the team's transporter, prior to a Winston Cup race.

A race mechanic can't be afraid to be on his back under a 3,500-pound race car to get the job done.

comfortable there because of the speeds and the injuries. I don't think a lot of people look forward to going there right now. I would like to see it slow down a bit."

The track may be shaped differently, but the pressure remains the same for any team that is hoping to clinch NASCAR's biggest prize—the Winston Cup title. "I don't enjoy the pressure," Evernham admitted. "I would rather let others on the crew take care of Atlanta while I go to Hawaii! No, I don't enjoy the pressure, not at all, but that is the sport. That is our job. In 1997, I don't think the pressure was any different on Jimmy Fennig (Mark Martin's crew chief) or Todd Parrott (Dale Jarrett's crew chief) or anybody else. Their whole season was coming down to that one race. I don't like it but that's my job and I have to deal with it."

Gordon said his crew chief may hate the pressure, but it's what the team has done earlier in the season that puts him in position to win championships. "In 1997, if one looks at how tight the battle was, there was definitely a lot of pressure on the line," Gordon said. "You feel like a big failure if you come out of that thing up in the points and only finish 17th. You either struggle to do it, or you don't do it. That is the worst situation you can be in, having to take that on your shoulders. To me, the best kind of pressure is trying to win something or going for a championship, and everybody is looking at whether you are going to do it when it comes down to that final event. It is tough on everybody, and there is not much room for mistakes. As much as Ray hates it, he is still really good at it. That is what counts. It doesn't matter how much you like it or not, it's how good you are at it. We've lived up to the pressure before. Desire and wanting it really bad mean a lot, but experience means a lot, too."

Although Gordon has won three of the last four NASCAR Winston Cup championships, his title clinchers have not always come in a blaze of glory. That was the feeling Evernham wanted with Gordon's title in 1998. He wanted to win a title in a decisive fashion, rather than outlasting the competition in the season finale. "That is something that is very important to me," Evernham admitted. "Hopefully, it will be this year or whatever. I want to leave Atlanta knowing we not only won the championship, but kicked butt in the race."

Evernham wants to experience what Bobby Labonte has enjoyed in three of the last four races at Atlanta Motor Speedway. Labonte won the 1996 NAPA 500 when older brother Terry clinched his second Winston Cup title. Bobby Labonte dominated the 1997 NAPA 500 by leading 163 laps and defeating Jarrett by 3.801 seconds. Evernham's anxiety began on the Saturday morning before the race, when Gordon spun his car on pit road and crashed into the STP Pontiac of Bobby Hamilton. That led Hamilton's team owner, Richard Petty, to quip, "I guess that proves the boy can't walk on water like I can."

Both drivers had to switch to backup cars, and neither was a factor in the race. Gordon, however, was able to limp to a 17th place finish, which allowed him to win the Winston Cup title by 14 points over Jarrett. Martin finished third in the season standings, 29 points behind Gordon and 15 behind Jarrett. While Gordon got to celebrate the title, Labonte had the only dominating performance of the day. "I don't know why I do so well there," Labonte said. "I think it is more of a combination. The 18 car ran good when Dale Jarrett was the driver. I think I ran good there before, too. Even though I had never won a race at either one of those places, I always had better finishes there than other places. When we all got together, we moved it a notch forward."

Richard Childress used to be in Evernham's position of enduring the pressure of a points race. He has owned cars that Dale Earnhardt has driven to six of his seven Winston Cup titles. Childress' cars have won seven races at Atlanta Motor Speedway, most recently when Earnhardt won the 1996 Primestar 500. "I don't really like the new layout. This is just one person's opinion," Childress said. "I think it is a good track for the spectators. Once the track wears in and you have a good,

Robert Yates, team owner for Dale Jarrett and Kenny Irwin Jr., is considered one of the top engine builders in NASCAR Winston Cup racing. *Photo by Jim Haines, courtesy of Indianapolis Motor Speedway*

two-groove race track to pass on, we will enjoy it a lot more. On the old race track, you could get up high and pass. Now, with these radial tires, everybody wants to run right on the bottom. It makes it very tough to pass at that race track. That is one reason why I favor the older style of track. It was more raceable and it was friendlier racing. There was more racing at Atlanta in March 1997 than there was the following November, because the track allowed you to do a little more. I think by the fall of 1998, maybe we'll be able to get back on it and race some like we did in the old days."

Larry McReynolds and David Smith prepare to bring Mike Skinner in for a pit stop during the Brickyard 400. *Photo by John Schmidt, courtesy of Indianapolis Motor Speedway*

Childress believes while the championship contenders have all the pressure, the rest of the field can take chances to get into victory lane at season's end. "At the end of the year, what makes it tough is that all the guys racing for points start doing all kinds of gambling and chasing," Childress said. "Back when we were winning championships, there were cars we were having to race those last five or six races that were trying to win races. Once you are out of the points, you try to win everything you can and take all the chances and gambles. If you are not in the points, you go down to Atlanta and hang it out those last five or six races. But if you are in the points, you can't afford the risk."

Bobby Labonte agrees with Childress. "You want to finish in the top 10, but if you don't have a chance to win, you may as well try something," Labonte said. "If you aren't in the top 10, you need to win a race. You can't be as conservative. In the chassis department or driver's department, I wouldn't know what to do differently if I went back there and was leading the points or running second in points."

Only one team will celebrate the championship, and only one team will get a chance to enjoy winning the season finale. But everybody in Winston Cup racing will get to enjoy a well-deserved break following the NAPA 500. "Two or three weeks after that, you are ready to go again," Labonte said. "At the same time, you know you can get regrouped. If you had a bad year, that can help you out. If you've had a good year, that can still help you out. If you go down there and win the race, you hope you can capitalize on it, and make the changes you need to make. There are so many things that add to that when you do win that race."

While the winning driver and team get to enjoy the rewards of their efforts, men like Evernham admit they

Todd Parrott, 34-year-old crew chief for Dale Jarrett, is one of the youngest crew chiefs in NASCAR Winston Cup racing. He is following in the footsteps of his father, Buddy Parrott, a longtime crew chief and currently general manager at Roush Racing.

are ready to collapse once the season is over. "The worst part is that a few days off doesn't really help you," Evernham said. "We are on a pretty wide-open, hectic schedule. You really don't get enough time to enjoy your accomplishments. That's a tough deal. You go through a postseason depression. You win the championship and you think, 'Wow, I'm going to go enjoy this.' Then you realize you have to get back right at it at the shop 12 hours a day in order to have a chance to win the Daytona 500. It's a tough grind. In the end, when you can kick back and take a look at it, everything is worth it, but there certainly is a postseason depression that happens after Atlanta."

In the ever-demanding world of NASCAR Winston Cup racing, success is ephemeral. When one season ends, it's time to get back to work in an attempt to win the Winston Cup title next season. After all, when the 1998 NAPA 500 is over, testing for the 1999 Daytona 500 is less than seven weeks away.

And a mechanic's work is never done.

Index